CHRISTOPH WILLIBALD GLUCK

Routledge Music Bibliographies

SERIES EDITOR: BRAD EDEN

COMPOSERS

Isaac Albéniz (1998)
Walter A. Clark

C. P. E. Bach (2002)
Doris Bosworth Powers

Samuel Barber (2001)
Wayne C. Wentzel

Béla Bartók (1997)
Second Edition
Elliott Antokoletz

Vincenzo Bellini (2002)
Stephen A. Willier

Alban Berg (1996)
Bryan R. Simms

Leonard Bernstein (2001)
Paul F. Laird

Johannes Brahms (2003)
Heather Platt

Benjamin Britten (1996)
Peter J. Hodgson

Elliott Carter (2000)
John L. Link

Carlos Chávez (1998)
Robert Parker

Frédéric Chopin (1999)
William Smialek

Aaron Copland (2001)
Marta Robertson and Robin
Armstrong

Josquin Des Prez (2004)
Carlo Fiore

Gaetano Donizetti (2000)
James P. Cassaro

Edward Elgar (1993)
Christopher Kent

Gabriel Fauré (1999)
Edward R. Phillips

Christoph Willibald Gluck
(2003)
Second Edition
Patricia Howard

Charles Ives (2002)
Gayle Sherwood

Scott Joplin (1998)
Nancy R. Ping-Robbins

Zoltán Kodály (1998)
Mícheál Houlahan and Philip
Tacka

Franz Liszt (2004)
Second Edition
Michael Saffle

Guillaume de Machaut (1995)
Lawrence Earp

Felix Mendelssohn Bartholdy
(2001)
John Michael Cooper

Giovanni Pierluigi da
Palestrina (2001)
Clara Marvin

Giacomo Puccini (1999)
Linda B. Fairtile

Maurice Ravel (2003)
Stephen Zank

Gioachino Rossini (2002)
Denise P. Gallo

Alessandro and Domenico
Scarlatti (1993)
Carole F. Vidali

Camille Saint-Saens (2003)
Timothy Flynn

Heinrich Schenker (2003)
Benjamin Ayotte

Jean Sibelius (1998)
Glenda D. Goss

Richard Strauss (2004)
Scott Warfield

Giuseppe Verdi (1998)
Gregory Harwood

Tomás Luis de Victoria (1998)
Eugene Casjen Cramer

Richard Wagner (2002)
Michael Saffle

Adrian Willaert (2003)
David Michael Kidger

GENRES

Central European Folk Music
(1996)
Philip V. Bohlman

Chamber Music (2002)
John H. Baron

Choral Music (2001)
Avery T. Sharp and James
Michael Floyd

Ethnomusicology (2003)
Jennifer Post

Jazz Research and
Performance Materials (1995)
Second Edition
Eddie S. Meadows

Music in Canada (1997)
Carl Morey

North American Indian Music
(1997)
Richard Keeling

Opera (2001)
Second Edition
Guy Marco

The Recorder (2003)
Second Edition
Richard Griscom and David
Lasocki

Serial Music and Serialism
(2001)
John D. Vander Weg

CHRISTOPH WILLIBALD GLUCK
A GUIDE TO RESEARCH
SECOND EDITION

PATRICIA HOWARD

ROUTLEDGE MUSIC BIOGRAPHIES
ROUTLEDGE
NEW YORK AND LONDON

Published in 2003 by
Routledge
29 West 35th Street
New York, NY 10001
www.routledge-ny.com

Published in Great Britain by
Routledge
11 New Fetter Lane
London EC4P 4EE
www.routledge.co.uk

Routledge is an imprint of the Taylor & Francis Group.
Printed in the United States of America on acid-free paper.

10 9 8 7 6 5 4 3 2 1

Library of Congress Cataloging-in-Publication Data
Howard, Patricia.
   Christoph Willibald Gluck : a guide to research / Patricia Howard.—
2nd ed.
      p. cm. — (Routledge music bibliographies)
Includes indexes.
   ISBN 0-415-94072-9 (hardcover : alk. paper)
   1. Gluck, Christoph Willibald, Ritter von, 1714–1787—Bibliography.
I. Title. II. Series: Routledge musical bibliographies.
   ML134.G56   H7   2003
   016.7821′092—dc21
                                                        2002153872

Contents

Preface to the Second Edition

The music of Christoph Willibald Gluck has generated a wealth of critical comment, polemic, analysis, and interpretation from the composer's lifetime to the present day: the ever-increasing body of Gluck literature reflects both changing taste in the theater and changing criteria of scholarship through more than two centuries. The last two decades have seen an unprecedented expansion of Gluck scholarship (accompanied by a welcome increase in performances of the music), and I am glad to have the opportunity to bring this bibliography up to date.

A list of the major available sources for a study of the music, including published and manuscript material, is set out in Chapter I. Chapter II offers a selection of primary sources dealing with the issues affecting all those working in the eighteenth-century theater, where subtle but enduring changes in the concept of music for the stage were taking place, of which Gluck's "reform" was only one among many initiatives. Chapter III covers a wide range of research material, principal among which are bibliographies and thematic catalogues, letters, and iconography; this chapter also includes surveys of research and pays tribute to notable past scholars; collections of essays, including the groundbreaking *Gluck-Jahrbuch*, are also listed here. The majority of secondary sources fall within Chapters IV, V, VI, and VII. Drawing upon a wide chronological range and diversity of styles, from the pioneering work of Anton Schmid (item 144 in the bibliography; all item numbers refer to entries in the bibliography) to the many excellent modern writers such as Bruce Alan Brown (item 166), Alessandra Martina (item 454), and Julian Rushton (item 469), I have aimed to prove that Gluck has in general been well served by those who have been attracted to study him and that, besides outstanding scholars of every generation, many fellow composers—Grétry (item 115), Salieri (item 143), Berlioz (item 293), Liszt (item 337), and Wagner (item 364)—have written both affectionately and perceptively about his music. A new section on the reception of Gluck's music has been added to Chapter V to include both reviews of the first performances and responses to the operas in subsequent centuries. Chapter VII surveys an area that is still underinvestigated. The aims and opinions of Gluck's librettists and choreographers are well documented, but we know tantalizingly little about the singers and designers, on whom fell a large share of the burden of interpreting his dramatic concept; information about production methods is still a rarity.

The bibliography is necessarily selective, more so than the first edition, since the quantity and quality of Gluck research has increased markedly in the fifteen years since the bicentenary of his death; in order to take account of as much modern research as possible, some items included in the first edition have been pruned. In selecting items for annotation, I have tried consciously to redress an imbalance, which has existed ever since Gluck's arrival in Paris in 1773, between the vast bulk of writing about the Paris operas, the considerably smaller quantity about the Viennese reform operas and ballets, and the scanty coverage of the early operas and other genres. To this end, I have included quite minor items dealing with the third category and have excluded much popular or derivative coverage of areas already soundly investigated in more scholarly studies. The only categories I have excluded on principle are reviews of performances where no profound discussion of the work itself takes place. I have restricted dictionary articles to two categories: those that include the earliest references to Gluck (Dlabač, item 105, Gerber, item 112, and Luca, item 130), and major modern musical encyclopedias, notably *Die Musik in Geschichte und Gegenwart* (item 91), and *New Grove (*item 99), whose articles constitute the best biographies currently available.

The entries are drawn from published material of all types, books, articles, and newspaper items, in English, French, German, and Italian. This edition was completed in August 2002. Since my plan was to include nothing unread (apart from a few unavailable dissertations), I have had to forego consideration of several dozen older items that appeared to promise attractive coverage of out-of-the-way topics (the accessibility of nineteenth-century newspapers is a particular problem). Those endowed with greater patience—or luck—than I can find items listed in the bibliographies in Chapter III.1, in particular Keller (item 44), and Wurzbach (item 50), which they may find it worthwhile to try to track down, and I would be particularly glad to hear of any important additions discovered in this way. At the other end of the chronological scale, new, enlightening investigations are being published almost monthly, and I am bound to have missed a few very recent articles that found their way into the bibliographical indexes too late for me to obtain copies of them. That such an abundance exists and is constantly increasing shows the healthy state of Gluck research in the twenty-first century.

I have received great courtesy and forbearance from a number of libraries. I should like to record my gratitude first to the library of the Open University, Milton Keynes, on whose advisory and search services I have surely made unprecedented demands. Particular thanks are also due to the staff of the Bibliothèque Nationale and Bibliothèque de l'Opéra in Paris, the Österreichische Nationalbibliothek and Gesellschaft der Musikfreunde in Vienna, the Staatsbibliothek in Berlin, the Fürst Thurn und Taxis Hofbibliothek in Regensburg, the Národní

Muzeum in Prague, the Civico Museo in Bologna, the Statensbibliothek in Stockholm, and the Pierpont Morgan Library in New York. In fact almost all the libraries listed in the Abbreviations section have responded to my requests, either in person or by correspondence, with exceptional efficiency and unfailing kindness. I owe a great debt to Daniela Philippi, Denise Gallo, and Brad Short for help in tracing Gluck autographs and to Neil Williams for picture searches. Finally, thanks are due to my family, who have zealously undertaken the work of unpaid research assistants while on their global travels.

Introduction

Writing within twenty years of the composer's death, Christian Schubart identified Gluck as one who "belonged to no school and who founded no tradition" (item 354). Two hundred years later this judgment still seems apt. It is Gluck's uniqueness that continues to fascinate: a Bohemian composer, trained in Italy, coming of age in Austria, who attained his finest achievements while satisfying the demanding audiences for French opera, Gluck's response to each environment was an individual one. His musical personality was already evident in his earliest operas for Milan and showed itself ever more strongly; while the last operas owed their external structures to French tradition, their emotional intensity arose from the composer's distinctive approach to dramatic narration. Gluck came remarkably close to fulfilling his declared intentions to produce "a music fit for all nations" and to eliminate "the ridiculous differentiation between national styles" (letter of February 1, 1773, in item 336). But the consistent vision, the single dramatic concept that unified his works produced in diverse dramatic traditions, also isolated him from his contemporaries. With the three composers who owe most to Gluck—Mozart, Berlioz, and Wagner—the debt was disguised by their even stronger personalities. Gluck's influence, which can be traced in details of method, mood, and orchestration in Mozart's operas and in an approach to large-scale structure in Berlioz and Wagner, is both too precise and too general to be called a "school."

In seeking to define Gluck's unique dramatic concept, his own writings are by no means to be taken as a straightforward guide. His avowed aim, to "restrict music to its true function of helping poetry to be expressive" (*Alceste* Preface), no more than echoes a common mid-eighteenth-century aesthetic (see, for example, items 1, 6, 12, and 35), though it appears more often from the pens of librettists and philosophers than musicians. A potential complication lies in the fact that we do not know the extent to which Gluck's prefaces and major artistic statements are his own composition: the *Alceste* Preface is generally acknowledged to have been drafted by Calzabigi. Gluck served well, having been on the whole well served by, his various librettists. There is little evident of conflict between the interests of word and music in his operas. Where, for example, in "O malheureuse

Iphigénie" (*Iphigénie en Tauride*), an opportunity for expansive lyricism arose, lyrical and even opulent melody was provided; where, in "Nò crudel, non posso vivere" (*Alceste*), anguished expression needed the precise use of vocal registers, Gluck made this his priority; where, on the other hand, the declamation of changing moods demanded a fluid approach, Gluck created an appropriate style, sensitive to the accentuation of the text and with the mood changes dictating the musical structure, as in "Brillant auteur de la lumière" (*Iphigénie en Aulide*). Furthermore, his willingness to respond to the needs of the poet did not inhibit him from reserving some of the most powerful dramatic moments to be portrayed by the orchestra: besides the celebrated soliloquy of Orestes in *Iphigénie en Tauride,* he also devised the much shorter but no less expressive instrumental introduction to Act II of the same opera and the masterly tone poem, "Che puro ciel!" in *Orfeo,* in which the voice is almost incidental to the orchestral texture.

The relationship between words and music formed the major crux of Gluck criticism in his lifetime. Forkel led the anti-Gluck camp, declaring that *Alceste* had "too much music to make good declamation, and too little music to be considered an opera" (item 311). In France the attack was taken up by La Harpe, who measured Gluck's vocal writing against definitions in the *Encyclopédie,* and found that his melodies lacked the balanced phrasing and self-sufficient structure advocated by Rousseau (in item 331). More trenchantly, La Harpe accused Gluck of devising an unconventional and individual style in order to hide his technical shortcomings (item 332).

The accusation stuck. Gluck's lack of Italianate lyricism is no longer a topic of modern criticism, but the simplicity of his language puzzled some critics writing well after Forkel. Handel's famous comment (in item 106) on Gluck's lack of contrapuntal ability proved to be as memorable as it is irrelevant, but Gluck's deliberately pared-down style became a stumbling block for a number of nineteenth-century musicians. Wagner's curious editing of *Iphigénie en Aulide* bears witness to one attempt to "rectify" this "fault" (in item 364). The debate is summarized in item 155, where Hermann Abert defended Gluck from Otto Jahn's assessment of his limited technique by arguing that this style was the result of the deliberate choice of a rationalist composer. Abert's case depends on Gluck's own declaration: "I considered that my greatest efforts should be concentrated on seeking a beautiful simplicity. I have avoided making a show of complexity at the expense of clarity" (*Alceste* Preface).

Paradoxically, Gluck's aim to free himself from the demands of his singers led him to evolve a style which, while being more vulnerable than most to inadequate performance, comes fully to life only in the theater, and this fact accounts for some of the swings of fortune his reputation has suffered: in times when his operas are frequently and enthusiastically performed, he is widely perceived to be among the greatest opera composers of his age. When his scores languish on library shelves, his achievements are invariably underestimated. No wonder critic after critic ends his study of the composer with a plea for more performances of the operas (items 80, 84, 126, etc.).

When Hermann Abert identified Gluck as a "rationalist" composer, he opened up one of the major areas of critical debate for the first half of the twentieth century. Abert argued that Gluck stood at a turning point in operatic history, between the aesthetic of *Affekt* that governed baroque opera and the theory of the Imitation of Nature that held sway in the classical period (items 156 and 157). He identified a tension in Gluck's developing style between characterization that offers a typical, appropriate representation of universal experience and that which draws an individual response to unique situations. Abert saw Gluck as remaining essentially on the conservative (baroque) side of the divide and attributed the term "rationalist" to him because he felt the composer was motivated primarily by dramatic theory—by a conscious engagement with the issues identified in Chapter II of this bibliography—and that this theory dictated the simplicity and clarity of this style. Abert's reading of Gluck was developed more fully by Walther Vetter (especially in item 212). The contrary view was advanced by Rudolf Gerber (item 317), who claimed that Gluck's position in history lay among the proto-Romantics: Gerber argued that Gluck's contemporaries saw him as an expressive composer rather than a theorist, insisting that he was influenced by *Sturm und Drang* models in literature and reacted to an intuitive consciousness of human nature rather than behaving according to acquired dramatic theory. Subsequently Wilhelm Baethge made the issue an ideological one, claiming Gluck as a hero of the "bourgeois ideals of the Enlightenment" (item 160); focusing on the act of the reform, he saw Gluck as a conscious revolutionary, and in dwelling on his realistic depiction of individuals, he shared Gerber's view of Gluck as an essentially modern composer. The debate continued in a lively exchange of views between Carl Dahlaus (items 426, 427), and Albrecht and Karin Stoll (item 478).

A further concern of modern scholarship has arisen from our more historically informed appreciation of late baroque opera. To the ever-relevant question of who was responsible for the reform of opera, Romain Rolland (item 561), was among the first to urge Metastasio's claim to be considered, on the basis of a letter from the librettist to Hasse. His view was attacked by Andrea della Corte (item 544), contesting Rolland's dependence on a single source by citing a wide-ranging selection of the writings, both of Metastasio and of his contemporaries, emphasizing Metastasio's fidelity to the conventions of traditional opera. While Della Corte's intention was to promote an appreciation of Calzabigi's role in the reform (especially in item 170), a reassessment by Paolo Gallarati advocates a more moderate view (items 548, 549). Gallarati concludes that Metastasio and Calzabigi represent different stages of a continuous historical development and that it is as easy to overestimate Calzabigi's commitment to the reform as it is to undervalue Metastasio's.

The reevaluation of Metastasian opera seria has tended to change the emphasis of studies of Gluck's youthful operas. Where earlier scholars were anxious to trace evidence of Gluck's reform tendencies in the Milan works (Abert, item 369, Arend, item 159, Vetter, item 403), later scholars found it unproblematic to show Gluck's early operas as thoroughly traditional (Hans Joachim Moser, item 190, and Anna Amalie Abert, item 92). Further lines of investigation, however, are suggested by Klaus Hortschansky's penetrating study (item 179) of Gluck's habit of self-borrowing, which he indulged in throughout his life. Hortschansky's study was arguably the most important contribution to Gluck studies in the second half of the twentieth century and yet it poses more questions than it answers, the principal among them being: How can Gluck's mature operas present the unity of style and dramatic method that they undoubtedly do while they can be shown to incorporate, often almost unchanged, material from a much earlier period of his development? Gluck studies, then, return continually to the starting point: the unique personality of the composer and its manifestation in his music.

Past research was dominated by the image of Gluck as reformer. The inquiry is not yet exhausted, for we now know far more about those genres that he "reformed" and indeed we are as likely to be able to find works by Handel (though not by Hasse, Traetta, or Jommelli) and Rameau (though not Boismortier or Mondonville) in the opera house and record catalogue as we are to find Gluck's own operas there. Closer acquaintance with Gluck's predecessors can only sharpen our perception of his debt to his immediate past and define more precisely his points of departure from it. While a more accurate knowledge of the genre of *festa teatrale* led Raymond Monelle (item 248) and Frederick Sternfeld (item 205) to advocate a reassessment of *Orfeo*—once viewed as the key manifestation of the reform, now identified as a transitional work standing between the prereform and the reform operas—it is no longer necessary to deplore or excuse Gluck's adherence to the baroque convention of the *lieto fine*, as Ludwig Finscher's thoughtful explorations have revealed (item 173). A better understanding of genre was one of the most generally useful achievements of the twentieth century, and Gluck studies have particularly benefited from this development.

Gluck's relationship to his inheritance is well-trodden though still fertile ground. His significance for the development of opera in the nineteenth century has been less extensively explored, despite the impassioned but imprecise Gluck-Wagner comparisons which flooded the bookshelves at the turn of the century. Perhaps we have taken Schubart's analysis too literally. Gluck may have "founded no tradition" but his achievements in the fields of characterization, orchestration, and the building of large-scale structures have left their mark on virtually all subsequent opera composers—that is, on opera itself. His stylistic fluidity, which merged aria and recitative into long stretches of *accompagnato* and dramatized the role of the chorus, was taken up in French, German, and even Italian opera in the nineteenth century. And his assertion of the primacy of the text led not so much to a new relationship between words and music, for the balance is a constantly shifting one, but rather to a new role for librettist. The eighteenth-century commonplace of a single libretto being passed from composer to composer gradually gave way to the idea of a unique match between a libretto and its setting.

Whether Gluck's influence on the course of operatic history can be more precisely defined remains to be proved. Since the first edition of this work, the activity of the *Sämtliche Werke* has been prodigious, making available, at time of writing, twenty-seven operas, two ballets, and the Trio Sonatas in useful editions of varying quality. There remain seven operas and one ballet complete in manuscript and a further ten operas of which only fragments exist. More performances of the earlier works, newly restored through the collected edition, will surely follow. Every new publication and, to an even greater degree, every new production, enriches our view of Gluck's genius and extend an irresistible invitation to both scholars and operagoers to deepen their acquaintance with the work of a unique dramatist.

Abbreviations

LIBRARY SIGLA

A-Gd	Austria, Graz, Diözesanarchiv
A-GÖ	Austria, Göttweig, Benediktinerstift Musikarchiv
A-KR	Austria, Kremsmünster, Benediktinerstift Musikarchiv
A-Wgm	Austria, Vienna, Gesellschaft der Musikfreunde
A-Wn	Austria, Vienna, Österreichische Nationalbibliothek
B-Bc	Belgium, Brussels, Conservatoire Royal de Musique
B-Br	Belgium, Brussels, Bibliothèque Royale Albert 1
CH-Bu	Switzerland, Basle, Universität Basel, Öffentliche Bibliothek, Musikabteilung
CH-BEl	Switzerland, Berne, Schweizerische Landesbibliothek
CH-CObodmer	Switzerland, Cologny-Geneva, Biblioteca Bodmeriana
CH-N	Switzerland, Neuchâtel, Bibliothèque publique et universitaire
CH-W	Switzerland, Wintherthur, Stadtbibliothek
CH-Zk	Switzerland, Zurich, Konservatorium und Musikhochschule
CZ-Bm	Czech Republic, Brno, Moravské Zemské Muzeum
CZ-BER	Czech Republic, Beroun, Statní Okresní Archiv
CZ-K	Czech Republic, Český Krumlov, Prakoviste Statniho Archivu Trebon
CZ-Pnm	Czech Republic, Prague, Národní Muzeum
D-ALT	Germany, Altenburg, Bibliothek des Landestheaters
D-Bsb	Germany, Berlin, Staatsbibliothek zu Preussischer Kulturbesitz
D-BDk	Germany, Brandenburg, Domstiftsarchiv und Bibliothek
D-Dlb	Germany, Dresden, Sächsische Landesbibliothek
D-DS	Germany, Darmstadt, Hessische Landes- und Hochschulbibliothek
D-F	Germany, Frankfurt am Main, Stadt- und Universitätsbibliothek
D-GOl	Germany, Gotha, Forschungs- und Landesbibliothek
D-Hs	Germany, Hamburg, Staats- und Universitätsbibliothek

D-Mbs	Germany, Munich, Bayerische Staatsbibliothek
D-MEI	Germany, Meiningen, Staatsliche Museen
D-MÜu	Germany, Münster, Westfälische Wilhelms-Universitätsbibliothek
D-Rtt	Germany, Regensburg, Fürst Thurn und Taxis Hofbibliothek
D-RUl	Germany, Rudolstadt, Thüringische Staatsarchiv
D-Sl	Germany, Stuttgart, Württembergische Landesbibliothek
D-WRdn	Germany, Weimar, Deutsches Nationaltheater und Staatskappelle Archiv
D-WRh	Germany, Weimar, Hochschule für Musik Franz Liszt
D-WRl	Germany, Weimar, Thüringische Hauptstaatsarchiv
D-WRtl	Germany, Weimar, Thüringische Landesbibliothek
DK-A	Denmark, Århus, Statsbiblioteket
DK-Kk	Denmark, Copenhagen, Kongelige Bibliotek
F-Pn	France, Paris, Bibliothèque Nationale
F-Po	France, Paris, Bibliothèque-Musée de l'Opéra
GB-Lbl	Great Britain, London, British Library
H-Bb	Hungary, Budapest, Bartók Béla Zenemüveszeti Szakközépiskola Könyvtár
H-Bn	Hungary, Budapest, Országos Széchényi Könyvtár
I-Bc	Italy, Bologna, Civico Museo Bibliografico Musicale
I-BGc	Italy, Bergamo, Biblioteca Civica Angelo Mai
I-BRc	Italy, Brescia, Conservatorio di Musica, A. Venturi
I-Fc	Italy, Florence, Conservatorio di Musica, Luigi Cherubini
I-Gl	Italy, Genoa, Conservatorio di Musica Nicolò Paganini
I-Mc	Italy, Milan, Conservatorio di Musica Giuseppe Verdi
I-MOe	Italy, Modena, Biblioteca Estense e Universitaria
I-Nc	Italy, Naples, Conservatorio di Musica, S. Pietro a Majella
I-Pca	Italy, Padua, Basilica del Santo, Biblioteca Antoniana
I-PAc	Italy, Parma, Conservatorio di Musica Arrigo Boito
I-PLcon	Italy, Palermo, Conservatorio di Musica Vincenzo Bellini
I-Rsc	Italy, Rome, Conservatorio di Musica S Cecilia
I-Tf	Italy, Turin, Accademia Filarmonica
I-Tn	Italy, Turin, Biblioteca Nazionale Universitaria
I-Vc	Italy, Venice, Conservatorio di Musica Benedetto Marcello
I-Vnm	Italy, Venice, Biblioteca Nazionale Marciana
NL-DHgm	Netherlands, The Hague, Haags Gemeentemuseum Musikafdeling
RUS-SPsc	Russia, St. Petersburg, Rossiyskaya Natsional'naya Biblioteka
S-L	Sweden, Lund, Universitetsbiblioteket
S-Skma	Sweden, Stockholm, Kungliga Musikaliska Akademiens Bibliothek

S-Smf	Sweden, Stockholm, Stiftelsen Musikkulturens Främjande
S-Uu	Sweden, Uppsala, Universitetsbiblioteket
S-Vx	Sweden, Växjö, Landsbiblioteket
US-AUS	USA, Austin, University of Texas
US-BEm	USA, Berkeley, University of California Music Library
US-NYpm	USA, New York, Pierpont Morgan Library
US-SLug	USA, St. Louis, Washington University, Gaylord Music Library
US-STum	USA, Stanford, Stanford Memorial Library
US-Wc	USA, Washington, Library of Congress, Music Division

EDITIONS

DTB	*Denkmäler deutscher Tonkunst, zweite Folge: Denkmäler der Tonkunst in Bayern*
DTÖ	*Denkmäler der Tonkunst in Österreich*
G	*Christoph Willibald Gluck: Sämtliche Werke*

Illustrations

Plate 1   Gluck, portrait by Jean-Silfrède Duplessis, 1775. Reproduced by permission of the Kunsthistorisches Museum, Vienna.

Plate 2   Autograph letter from Gluck to Franz Kruthoffer, dated Vienna, August 30, 1780. Reproduced by permission of the Pierpont Morgan Library.

Plate 3   Fragment of an autograph letter from Gluck to Anne Pierre Jacques de Vismes de Valgay, dated Vienna, April 1, 1778. The original of the letter is in the possession of the Bibliothèque Nationale, Paris.

Plate 4   Opening page of the autograph score of *Armide*, 1777. Reproduced by permission of the Neil Williams Classical Collection. The original score is in the possession of the Bibliothèque de l'Opéra, Paris.

Gluck, oil painting by Jean-Silfrède Duplessis, 1775. Reproduced by permission of the
Kunsthistorisches Museum, Vienna.

Autograph letter from Gluck to Franz Kruthoffer, dated Vienna, August 30, 1780. The Mary Flagler Cary Music Collection in the Pierpont Morgan Library, MFC G 5675. Reproduced by permission of the Pierpont Morgan Library.

Photographic copy of a fragment of an autograph letter from Gluck to Anne Pierre Jacques de Vismes de Valgay, dated Vienna, April 1, 1778, reproduced in item 154, where the handwriting is analyzed by Louis Vauzanges. The original of the letter is in the possession of the Bibliothèque Nationale, Paris.

Photographic copy of the opening of the first act of *Armide* (Paris 1777, text by Quinault): page 1 from the fragment that has been preserved of the autograph score. The original fragment is in the possession of the Bibliothèque de l'Opéra, Paris. Photograph: The Neil Williams Classical Collection.

I

The Compositions

1. A LIST OF GLUCK'S COMPOSITIONS

This list is based on the work list in *New Grove* (item 99). For published works, reference is made to the *Sämtliche Werke* (G), where available, or to earliest and most recent published editions; the reader is referred to Hopkinson (item 43) for library locations of some of the rarer printed material. A selection of manuscript copies of the published works is also listed, since these often afford useful information about local or variant productions. For the unpublished works or where no reliable modern edition exists, manuscript sources are given; for partially surviving operas, every known number is identified, and by including arias borrowed from earlier works or incorporated into later works (following Hortschansky, item 179), it has been possible to expand the tally of known arias in the early operas, though it is of course impossible to establish the degree of reworking that may have taken place. Publication data for the librettos are added where known. Numbers assigned to the work list are for the purpose of cross-reference only and have no cataloguing significance. The entries in each section are arranged chronologically in the following format: title and genre; authorship and publication data of libretto; town, theater, and date of first performance; the extent and availability of the source material.

The Operas

1. *Artaserse. Dramma per musica* in three acts, libretto by Pietro Metastasio, Milan: Malatesta, 1741. Milan, Regio Ducal, Dec. 26, 1741. Two arias extant: "Mi scacci sdegnato," in ms in A-Wgm; "Se del fiume" in ms in B-Bc, CH-BEl, GB-Lbl.

2. *Demetrio (Cleonice)*. *Dramma per musica* in three acts, libretto by Metastasio, Venice: Rosetti, 1742. Venice, Grimani di San Samuele, May 2, 1742. Seven arias extant: "Misero non è tanto" in ms in B-Bc, F-Pn; "Se fecondo e vigoroso" in ms in B-Bc, F-Pn; "Scherza il nocchier talora" in ms in A-Wn, B-Bc, F-Pn; "Dal suo gentil sembiante" in ms in B-Bc, F-Pn; "Non so frenare il pianto" in ms in I-Bc; "Io so qual pena sia": in ms in S-Uu, ed. Max Arend, in DTB, Bd. 26, Jahrgang 14/2; "Quel labbro adorato" in ms in B-Bc, F-Pn.

3. *Demofoonte*. *Dramma per musica* in three acts, libretto by Metastasio, Milan: Malatesta, 1742. Milan, Regio Ducal, Jan. 6, 1743. Vocal score of Act I, ed. Julien Tiersot, Leipzig: Gluckgesellschaft vol. 1, 1914; all closed numbers except for sinfonia and one aria extant in ms in B-Bc, CH-BEl, F-Pn; single numbers in ms in A-Wn, D-Bsb, D-Dlb, I-Mc, I-Nc, US-Wc.

4. *Il Tigrane*. *Dramma per musica* in three acts, libretto by Francesco Silvani after Carlo Goldoni (*La virtù trionfante*), Brescia: Rizzardi, 1743. Crema, Sept. 26, 1743. Eleven arias and one duet extant: "Troppo ad un alma è caro" in ms in B-Bc, CH-BEl, F-Pn; "Vezzi, lusinghe" in ms in B-Bc, CH-BEl, F-Pn; "Se spunta amica stella" in ms in B-Bc, CH-BEl, F-Pn; "Sì, ben mio, morrò" in ms in B-Bc, CH-BEl, F-Pn, S-Vx; "Nero turbo il ciel" in ms in B-Bc, CH-BEl, F-Pn (a sacred parody of this aria in DK-Kk); "Se in grembo" in ms in B-Bc, CH-BEl, F-Pn; "Parto da te" in ms in B-Bc, CH-BEl, F-Pn; "Priva del caro" in ms in B-Bc, CH-BEl, F-Pn; "Care pupille amate" in ms in B-Bc, CH-BEl, F-Pn; "Lungi da te" (duet) in ms in B-Bc, CH-BEl, F-Pn; "Rasserena il mesto ciglio" in ms in B-Bc, CH-BEl, F-Pn; "Presso l'onda d'Acheronte" in ms in B-Bc, CH-BEl, F-Pn.

5. *La Sofonisba*. *Dramma per musica* in three acts, libretto by Silvani (recitatives) and Metastasio (arias), Milan: Malatesta, 1744. Milan, Regio Ducal, Jan. 18, 1744. Twelve arias and one duet extant: "Nobil onda" in ms in CH-BEl, F-Pn; "Se tanto piace" in ms in CH-BEl, F-Pn; "Tornate sereni" in ms in A-Wgm, reworked as "Perchè viva felice" in *La contesa de' numi* (see Hortschansky, item 179); "Se in campo armato" in ms in B-Bc, CH-BEl, F-Pn; "Non vi piacque" in ms in B-Bc, CH-BEl, F-Pn; "Tremo fra dubbi" in ms in CH-BEl, F-Pn; "Cara, dagli occhi tuoi" in ms in B-Bc, CH-BEl, F-Pn; "O frangi i lacci miei" in ms in CH-BEl, F-Pn; "È maggiore d'ogn'altro dolore" in ms in B-Bc, CH-BEl, F-Pn; "M'opprime, m'affanna" in ms in B-Bc, CH-BEl, F-Pn; "È sorta di tormento" reworked as "È uguale" in *La caduta de' giganti* (see Hortschansky, item 179); "Se fedel, cor mio" (duet) in ms in B-Bc, CH-BEl, F-Pn; "Là sul margine" in ms in CH-BEl, F-Pn.

6. *Ipermestra*. *Dramma per musica* in three acts, libretto by Metastasio, n.p., 1744. Venice, San Giovanni Grisostomo, Nov. 21, 1744. G iii/6, ed. Axel

Beer, 1997; ms copy in GB-Lbl; substantial excerpts in ms in I-MO; autograph score of sinfonia in CH-B (private collection).

7. *Poro. Dramma per musica* in three acts, libretto by Metastasio (*Alessandro nell'Indie*), Turin: Zappata, 1745. Turin, Regio, Dec. 26, 1744. Sinfonia, one duet, and four arias extant: sinfonia in ms in CZ-Pnm, I-Tf; "Se mai turbo" (duet) in ms in I-Tf; "Senza procella ancora" ed. Robert Haas (item 387); "Se viver non poss'io" in ms in A-Wn, I-Tf, ed. Haas (item 387); "Di rendermi la calma" in ms in I-Tf; "Son confusa pastorella" in ms in I-Tf.

8. *Ippolito. Dramma per musica* in three acts, libretto by Gioseffo Gorino Corio, Milan: Malatesta, 1745. Milan, Regio Ducal, Jan. 31, 1745. Eight arias and one duet extant: "Varca il mar" in ms in B-Bc, F-Pn; "Se tu vedessi" in ms in B-Bc, F-Pn; "Agitata non trovo riposo" partially transcribed by Hortschansky (item 392); "Non so placar mio sdegno" ed. Abert (item 368); "Parto, ma un giorno amore" in ms in B-Bc, F-Pn; "Chi noto mi fa" in ms in B-Bc, F-Pn; "Ah, m'ingannasti" (duet) in *La caduta de'giganti*, see below; "Ah già parmi che d'armi" in ms in B-Bc, F-Pn; "Dirai all'idol mio" in ms in B-Bc, F-Pn.

9. *La caduta de'giganti. Dramma per musica* in three acts, libretto by Francesco Vanneschi, London: n.p., 1745. London, King's Theatre, Jan. 7, 1746. Five arias and one duet in *The Favourite Songs in the Opera called La Caduta de'Giganti*, London: Walsh, 1746; four more arias borrowed from earlier operas (see Hortschansky, item 179): "Care pupille" in Walsh; "Vezzi, lusinghe" in Walsh; "Conserva a noi" in Walsh; "Tornate sereni" in *La Sofonisba*; "Se in grembo" in *Il Tigrane*; "Ah, m'ingannasti" (duet) in Walsh; "Pensa che il ciel trema" in *Ipermestra*; "Mai l'amor mio" in *Ipermestra*; "Sì, ben mio" in Walsh; "È uguale ad un tormento" in Walsh.

10. *Artamene. Dramma per musica* in three acts, libretto by Vanneschi, after Bartolommeo Vitturi, London: n.p., 1746. London, King's Theatre, Mar. 4, 1746. Six arias in *The Favourite Songs in the Opera called Artamene*, London: Walsh, 1746; nine further numbers borrowed from earlier operas (see Hortschansky, item 179): "Se crudeli" in Walsh, closing section in autograph in A-Wgm; "Se in campo armato" in *La Sofonisba*; "È maggiore d'ogni altro dolore" in Walsh; "T'intendo ingrato" in *Demofoonte*; "Il suo leggiadro viso" in Walsh; "Nobil onda" in *La Sofonisba*; "Non vi piacque" in *La Sofonisba*; "Troppo ad un alma è caro" in *Il Tigrane*; "Pensa a serbarmi" in Walsh; "O sciogli i lacci miei" in *La Sofonisba*; "Or del tuo re" in *Ipermestra*; "Se fedel cor mio" (duet) in *La Sofonisba*; "Rasserena il mesto ciglio" in Walsh; "Per lei fra le armi" in *Demofoonte*; "Presso l'onda d'Acheronte" in *Il Tigrane*; "Già presso al termine" in Walsh, opening section in autograph in A-Wgm.

11. *Le nozze d'Ercole e d'Ebe. Festa teatrale* in two acts, librettist unknown, libretto published Dresden: n.p., 1747. Pillnitz, Dresden, June 29, 1747. Ed. Abert in DTB Bd. 26, Jahrgang 14/2, 1914. M4 D4; in ms in B-Bc, D-Dlb.

12. *La Semiramide riconosciuta. Dramma per musica* in three acts, libretto by Metastasio, Vienna: van Ghelen, 1748. Vienna, Burgtheater, May 14, 1748. G iii/12, ed. Gerhard Croll & Thomas Hauschka, 1994; in ms in A-Wn (pub. in facsimile New York: Garland, 1982), D-Bsb, D-MEI.

13. *La contesa de'numi. Festa teatrale* in two acts, libretto by Metastasio, missing. Copenhagen, Charlottenborg, Apr. 9, 1749. In ms in B-Bc, DK-Kk; excerpts in CH-BEl, D-Bsb, F-Pn, I-Fc.

14. *Ezio. Dramma per musica* in three acts, libretto by Metastasio. Prague: Pruscha, 1750[?]. Prague, Kotzen, carnival, 1750. G iii/14, ed. Gabriele Buschmeier & Hanspeter Bennwitz, 1990; in ms in B-Bc, D-Bsb, D-Dlb, D-Sl, F-Pn, GB-Lbl; autograph of "Ecco alle mie catene" in D-Bsb.

15. *Issipile. Dramma per musica* in three acts, libretto by Metastasio, Prague: Pruscha, 1752[?]. Prague, Carnival, 1752. Possibly six arias and one duet extant: "Impallidisce in campo" reworked as "D'altre nubi è il sol" in *L'innocenza*; "Oh Dei, piegato un cor" (taken from "Oh Dei, che dolce incanto," in ms in D-Bsb, D-Dl, doubtful, see Hortschansky, item 179); "Ogni amante" reworked as "Se al impero" in *La clemenza*; "Ombra diletta" in ms in B-Bc, CH-BEl, GB-Lbl; "Parto, se vuoi così" in autograph in A-Wn, ms copy in CH-BEl; "Io ti lascio" in ms in B-Bc, CH-BEl, GB-Lbl; "Care luci" (duet, reworked as "Ah pietà", in ms in B-Bc, D-Bsb; doubtful, see Hortschansky, item 179).

16. *La clemenza di Tito. Dramma per musica* in three acts, libretto by Metastasio, missing. Naples, San Carlo, Nov. 4, 1752. G iii/16, ed. Franz Giegling, 1995; in ms in I-Nc; substantial excerpts in F-Pn, I-Mc.

17. *Le cinesi. Componimento drammatico* in one act, libretto by Metastasio, missing. Vienna, Schlosshof, Sept. 24, 1754. G iii/17, ed. Croll, 1958; in ms in D-Bsb, D-Dlb.

18. *La danza. Componimento drammatico pastorale* in one act, libretto by Metastasio, Vienna: n.p., 1755. Laxenburg, May 5, 1755. G iii/18, ed. Croll, 1969; in ms in A-Wn, CH-N, I-MO.

19. *L'innocenza giustificata. Festa teatrale* in one act, libretto by Giacomo Durazzo (recitatives) and Metastasio (arias), Vienna: van Ghelen, 1755.

Vienna, Burgtheater, Dec. 8, 1755. G iii/19, ed. Josef-Horst Lederer, 1999; in ms in A-Wgm, A-Wn, D-Bsb, DK-Kk, F-Pn.

20. *Antigono*. *Dramma per musica* in three acts, libretto by Metastasio, Rome: Amidei, 1756. Rome: Torre Argentina, Feb. 9, 1756. G iii/20, in preparation; in ms in B-Bc, CH-BEl, F-Pn, I-Mc.

21. *Il re pastore*. *Dramma per musica* in three acts, libretto by Metastasio, Vienna: van Ghelen, 1756. Vienna, Burgtheater, Dec. 8, 1756. G iii/8, ed. Lázló Somfai, 1968; in ms in A-Wn; substantial excerpts in A-KR, H-Bn.

22. *La fausse esclave*. *Opéra-comique* in one act, libretto after Louis Anseaume and Pierre de Marcouville, missing. Vienna, Burgtheater, Jan. 8, 1758. Complete except for sinfonia in ms in A-Wn, B-Bc, D-Dsb, F-Pn.

23. *L'île de Merlin, ou Le mond renversé*. *Opéra-comique* in one act. Libretto by Anseaume after Alain-René Lesage and D'Orneval, Vienna: van Ghelen, 1758. Vienna, Schönbrunn, Oct. 3, 1758. G iv/1, ed. Günter Hausswald, 1956; in ms in A-Wn, B-Bc, GB-Lbl, F-Pn.

24. *La Cythère assiégée*. *Opéra-comique* in one act, libretto by Charles-Simon Favart, Mannheim: n.p., 1759. Vienna, Burgtheater, Spring 1759. In ms in A-Wn, B-Bc, CZ-K, H-Bn; for sinfonia, see Arend (item 487).

25. *Le diable à quatre, ou Le double metamorphose*. *Opéra-comique* in three acts, libretto by Michel-Jean Sedaine and Pierre Baurans, after Charles Coffey (*The Devil to Pay*), Vienna: van Ghelen, 1759. Laxenburg, May 28, 1759. G iv/3, ed. Bruce Alan Brown, 1992; in ms in CZ-K, D-Dlb, D-Rtt, I-Vc.

26. *L'arbe enchanté, ou Le tuteur dupé*. *Opéra-comique* in one act, libretto after Jean-Joseph Vadé, *Le poirier*, Vienna: van Ghelen, 1759. Vienna, Schönbrunn, Oct. 3, 1759. In ms in A-Wn, B-Bc, F-Po; sinfonia in D-Rtt.

27. *Tetide*. Serenata in two acts, libretto by Giovanni Ambrogio Migliavacca, Vienna: van Ghelen, 1760. Vienna, Hofburg, Oct. 10, 1760. G iii/22, ed. Somfai, 1978; in ms in A-Wn, I-Tn.

28. *L'ivrogne corrigé*. *Opéra-comique* in two acts, libretto by Anseaume and Jean-Baptiste Lourder de Sarterre, Vienna: van Ghelen, 1760. Vienna, Burgtheater, late 1760. G iv/5, ed. Franz Rühlmann, 1951; in ms in B-Bc, D-Dlb.

29. *Le cadi dupé. Opéra-comique* in one act, libretto after Pierre-René Le Monnier, Paris: Duchesne, 1761. Vienna, Burgtheater, Dec. 9, 1761. G iv/6, ed. Daniela Philippi, 1999; in ms in A-Wn, CZ-K, D-Bsb, D-Hs, D-Rtt.

30. *Orfeo ed Euridice. Azione teatrale* in three acts, libretto by Ranieri de'Calzabigi, Vienna: van Ghelen, 1762. Vienna, Burgtheater, Oct. 5, 1762. Paris: Duchesne, 1764; G i/1, ed. Anna Amalie Abert & Ludwig Finscher, 1963; rejected autograph sketch of finale ("Trionfi amore") in A-Wn; many 18th-c ms copies including examples in A-Wgm, A-Wn, F-Pn, F-Po, GB-Lbl. See also Eitner (item 39).

31. *Il trionfo di Clelia. Dramma per musica* in three acts, libretto by Metastasio, Lucca: Vale, 1762. Bologna, Teatro Communale, May 14, 1763. G iii/23, in preparation; in ms in B-Bc, CH-BEl, D-Bsb, F-Pn; autograph of sinfonia in F-Po.

32. *Ezio. Dramma per musica* in three acts, revision of no. 14. Libretto by Metastasio, Vienna: van Ghelen, n.d. Vienna, Burgtheater, Dec. 26, 1763. G iii/24, ed. Buschmeier, 1992; in ms in CZ-Pnm.

33. *La rencontre imprévue. Opéra-comique* in three acts, libretto by Louis Hurtaut Dancourt after Lesage and d'Orneval, *Les pélerins de la Mecque*, Vienna: van Ghelen, 1763. Vienna, Burgtheater, Jan. 7, 1764. G iv/7, ed. Harald Heckmann, 1964; in ms in A-GÖ, A-Wn, B-Br, CZ-K, D-Dlb, F-Pn, NL-DHgm, S-Skma.

34. *Il Parnaso confuso. Azione teatrale* in one act, libretto by Metastasio, Vienna: van Ghelen, 1765. Vienna, Schönbrunn, Jan. 24, 1765. G iii/25, ed. Croll, 1974; in ms in A-KR, A-Wn, D-Dlb, F-Pn, I-MO, I-Nc.

35. *Telemaco ossia L'isola di Circe. Dramma per musica* in two acts, libretto by Marco Coltellini after Sigismondo Capece, Vienna: van Ghelen, 1765. Vienna, Burgtheater, Jan. 30, 1765. G i/2, ed. Karl Geiringer, 1972; ms copies in A-GÖ, A-Wgm, A-Wn, B-Br, D-Bsb, F-Pn, GB-Lbl, I-Nc; autograph fragment of Act I, scn 1 in A-Wn.

36. *La corona. Azione teatrale* in one act, libretto by Metastasio, never printed. Composed for Oct. 4, 1765 but not performed. G iii/26, ed. Croll, 1974; in ms in A-Wgm, A-Wn, B-Br, I-Nc.

37. *Il prologo. Prologue to Traetta's Ifigenia in Tauride*, for soprano solo, chorus, and orchestra, libretto by Lorenzo Ottavio del Rosso, n.p., 1767. Florence, Teatro di via della Pergola, Feb. 22, 1767. Ed. Paul Graf Waldersee, Leipzig: Breitkopf & Härtel, 1891.

38. *Alceste*. *Tragedia* in three acts, libretto by Calzabigi, Vienna: van Ghelen, 1767. Vienna, Burgtheater, Dec. 26, 1767. Vienna: Trattnern, 1769; G i/3 a, ed. Rudolf Gerber, 1957; i/3 b in preparation; ms copies in B-Br, D-GOl, D-Hs, D-RUl, D-WRdn, D-WRtl, I-BGc, I-BRc, I-Mc, I-Nc; autograph of "Misero! e che farò?" in GB-Lbl.

39. *Le feste d'Apollo*. *Festa teatrale* in prologue and three acts, libretto by Carlo Innocenzo Frugoni, Giuseppe Maria Pagnini, Giuseppe Pezzana, and Ranieri de'Calzabigi, Parma: Stamperia Reale, 1769. Parma, Corte, Aug. 24, 1769. G iii/28 a, b, in preparation; in ms in B-Bc, CH-BEl, D-Bsb, F-Pn, I-Nc, I-Pac; autograph fragment of chorus, "Eccheggiar s'odano" (*Atto d'Aristeo*) in A-Wgm.

40. *Paride ed Elena*. *Dramma per musica* in five acts, libretto by Calzabigi, Vienna: van Ghelen, 1770. Vienna, Burgtheater, Nov. 3, 1770. Vienna: Trattnern, 1770; G i/4, ed. Gerber, 1954; in ms in A-KR, D-DS, I-Mc, I-Nc.

41. *Iphigénie en Aulide*. *Tragédie opéra* in three acts, libretto by François-Louis Gand Leblanc du Roullet after Jean Racine, Paris: Delormel, 1774. Paris, Académie Royale, Apr. 19, 1774; Paris: Lemarchand, 1774; G i/5 a, b, ed. Marius Flothius, 1987; in ms in CH-Zk, D-ALT, D-BDk, F-Po, H-Bb, I-BGc, I-Nc, S-Skma.

42. *Orphée et Eurydice*. *Tragédie opéra* in three acts, revision of no. 30, libretto by Pierre-Louis Moline after Calzabigi, Paris: Delormel, 1774. Paris, Académie Royale, Aug. 2, 1774. Paris: Lemarchand, 1774; G i/6, ed. Finscher, 1967; substantial autograph excerpts in F-Pn and F-Po; other autograph fragments in D-Bsb, S-Smf, RUS-SPsc, US-STum.

43. *L'arbre enchanté*. *Opéra-comique* in one act, revision of no. 26, libretto by Moline, after Vadé, Paris: Lemarchand, 1775. Versailles, Feb. 27, 1775. Paris: Lemarchand, 1775. G iv/11, in preparation; autograph score in F-Pn.

44. *La Cythère assiégée*. *Opéra-ballet* in three acts, revision of no. 24, libretto by Favart, published Paris: Delormel, 1775. Paris, Académie Royale, Aug. 1, 1775. Paris: Bureau d'Abonnement Musical, [1775]; ed. Karl Mayer, Berlin: Bloch Erben, 1928 (vocal score); in ms in F-Po.

45. *Alceste*. *Tragédie opéra* in three acts, revision of no. 38, libretto by Du Roullet after Calzabigi, Paris: Delormel, 1776. Paris, Académie Royale, Apr. 23, 1776. Paris: Bureau d'Abonnement Musical, 1776; G i/7, ed. Gerber, 1957; autograph score in F-Pn; autograph fragments in CH-Bu (doubtful) and D-Bsb; ms copies in F-Po, S-Skma.

46. *Armide. Drame héroique* in five acts, libretto by Philippe Quinault, Paris: Delormel, 1777. Paris, Académie Royale, Sept. 23, 1777. Paris: Bureau d'Abonnement Musical, 1777; G i/8 a, b, ed. Klaus Hortschansky, 1991; substantial autograph excerpts in F-Pn, F-Po.

47. *Iphigénie en Tauride. Tragédie* in four acts, libretto by Nicolas-François, Guillard and Du Roullet, Paris: Delormel, 1779. Paris, Académie Royale, May 18, 1779. Paris: Bureau du Journal de Musique, 1779; G i/9, ed. Croll, 1973; in ms in F-Po (with autograph corrections by Gluck), H-Bb, I-Mc, S-St.

48. *Écho et Narcisse. Drame lyrique* in prologue and three acts, libretto by Baron Jean-Baptiste-Louis-Théodore de Tschoudi de Colombey, after Ovid, Paris: Delormel, 1779. Paris, Académie Royale, Sept. 24, 1779. Paris: Des Lauriers, [1781]; G i/10, ed. Gerber, 1953; in ms in A-Wgm, F-Pn, F-Po, S-Skma (incomplete); autograph fragment of final ballet in CH-CObodmer.

49. *Iphigenie auf Tauris* (*Iphigenie in Tauris*). *Tragisches Singspiel* in four acts, revision of no. 47, libretto by Johann Baptiste von Alxinger and Gluck, after Guillard and Du Roullet, Vienna: Logenmeister, 1781. Vienna, Burgtheater, Oct. 23, 1781. G i/11, ed. Croll, 1965; in ms in A-Wn, A-Wgm, CZ-Bm, D-SL; autograph fragment of vocal lines from IV4-6 in D-Bsb; autograph fragment of vocal lines in US-NYpm.

Pasticcios, Doubtful, and Missing Operas

50. *Arsace. Dramma per musica,* libretto by Antonio Salvi. Milan, Regio Ducal, Dec. 26, 1743. Eight arias in ms in B-Bc, F-Pn, of which "Perfido, traditore" and "Se fido l'adorai" are probably by Gluck; see Hortschansky (items 179 and 388).

51. *La finta schiava. Dramma per musica* compiled by Giacomo Maccari, libretto by Silvani. Venice, S. Angelo, May 13, 1744. Possibly three arias by Gluck: "Troppo ad un alma è caro" in *Il Tigrane* in ms in A-Wn, B-Bc, CZ-K, I-Tn; "Ch'io mai vi possa" in ms in B-Bc, F-Pn; "Se spunta amica stella" in *Il Tigrane*, in ms in B-Bc, F-Pn, CH-BEl; see Hortschansky (item 179).

52. *Tircis et Doristée, ou La vengeance inutile. Opéra-comique* in one act, libretto by Favart, after Ovid, missing. Laxenburg, May 10, 1756. Three arias probably by Gluck: "Je vois tomber" (from *L'innocenza giustificata*, "Quercia annosa"), "Dors, aimable Aurore," and "La chute d'un torrent," both in ms in A-Wn, CZ-K, I-Tn; see Brown (item 166).

53. *Le caprice amoureux, ou Ninette à la cour. Opéra-comique* in two acts, libretto by Favart after Goldoni (*Bertoldo, Bertoldino, e Cacasenno*), Vienna, Burgtheater, 1760. Two arias probably by Gluck: "Qu'il est bien de son village" and "Son exercise est ce qu'il faut," both in ms in A-Wn, I-Tn; see Brown (item 166).

54. *Arianna. Dramma per musica* in one act, libretto by Migliavacca, Vienna: van Ghelen, 1762. Laxenburg, May 27, 1762. Music lost, see Hortschansky (item 391).

55. *Enea e Ascanio. Componimento per musica,* libretto, Vienna: van Ghelen, 1764. Frankfurt am Main, Apr. 1764. Doubtful, music lost; see Hortschansky (item 179).

56. *Isabelle et Gertrud. Opéra-comique* in one act, libretto by Favart. Paris, Théâtre Italien, Aug. 14, 1765. Three arias possibly by Gluck: "Sans souci vivre pour soi" (from "Les hommes pieusement" in *La rencontre imprévue*), "Comme une rose" (from "A ma maîtresse" in *La rencontre imprévue*), "Rompons ensemble" in ms in D-Dlb; see Brown (item 489).

57. *La vestale. Festa teatrale* in two acts, revision of no. 19. Vienna: van Ghelen, 1768. Vienna, Burgtheater, Summer 1768. Music lost; see Einstein (item 381).

58. *Orfeo. Pasticcio,* libretto by Giovanni Botarelli, London: Griffin, 1770. Revision of no. 30, with additional music by J. C. Bach, Pietro Guglielmi, and Gaetano Guadagni. London, King's Theatre, April 7, 1770. *The Favourite Songs in the Opera "Orfeo,"* London: Bremner, 1770. Many subsequent versions based on this; see Howard (item 446), Robinson (item 466), and Cattelan (item 565).

59. *Die zwei Königinnen. Tragedia,* libretto by Karl Joseph von Pauersbach. Salzburg, Jan. 19, 1776. Doubtful, music lost; see Deutsch (item 305).

Secular Vocal Music

60. *Klopstocks Oden und Lieder beym Clavier zu Singen.* Lieder, words by Friedrich Gottlob Klopstock. 1. "Vaterlandslied," 2. "Wir und Sie," 3. "Schlachtgesang," 4. "Der Jüngling," 5. "Die Sommernacht," 6. "Die frühen Gräber," 7. "Die Neigung." Vienna: Artaria, 1785; in ms in B-Bc; nos. 2 & 3, ed. Johann Christoph Diederich, *Göttinger Musenalmanach*, 1774; earlier version of No. 4, ed. Diederich, *Göttinger Musenalmanach*, 1775; second version of No. 5, ed. Johann Heinrich Voss, *Vossischen Musenalmanach* (Ham-

burg), 1785; No. 6, ed. Diederich, *Göttinger Musenalmanach*, 1775. All nine Lieder ed. Gustav Beckmann, Leipzig: Gluckgesellschaft vol. 3, 1917.

61. *Ode an den Tod*. Lied, words by Klopstock, ed. Johann Friedrich Reichardt, in *Musikalischer Blumenstrauss*, Berlin, 1792; ed. Josef Liebeskind in *Ergänzungen und Nachträge* (in item 49).

62. "Minona, lieblich und hold." Duet, author unknown, ed. Reichardt in *Musikalische Blumenlese*, Berlin, 1795. Incipit in Hopkinson (item 43).

63. "Siegsgesang für Freie." Lied, words by Franz Matthisson, ed. Voss, in *Musenalmanach*, 1795. Incipit in Hopkinson (item 43).

New Grove (item 99) gives details of several more secular vocal numbers of doubtful ascription. Unattributed arias exist in ms in A-Wgm, A-Wn, B-Bc, D-Bsb, D-Dlb, F-Pn, S-Skma, US-AUS.

Sacred Vocal Music

64. Miserere. Eight-part chorus? Turin, 1744–1745; music lost.

65. Psalm VIII. Vienna, 1753–1757; music lost.

66. "Grand chœur." For three solo voices and chorus, performed Vienna, Mar. 18, 1762; music lost.

67. "Alma sedes." Motet for solo voice and orchestra. Paris: Lemarchand, before 1779. Incipit in Hopkinson (item 43).

68. De profundis. Motet for chorus and orchestra, performed at Gluck's funeral, Vienna, Nov. 17, 1787. Paris: A L'Imprimerie du Conservatoire de Musique, [1804]. Ed. Arend, Hamlin: Oppenheimer, 1915.

New Grove (item 99) gives details of three doubtful motets; a number of arias in Latin, adapted from operatic arias, exist in ms in A-Wn and DK-Kk.

Ballets

69. *Les amours de Flore et Zéphire*. Scenario by Gasparo Angiolini, missing. Vienna, Schönbrunn, Aug. 13, 1759. In ms in CZ-K; see Brown (item 166).

70. *Le naufrage*. Scenario by Angiolini, missing. Vienna, ?Burgtheater, 1759. In ms in CZ-K; see Brown (item 166).

71. *La halte des Calmouckes.* Scenario by Angiolini, missing. Vienna, Burgtheater, Mar. 23, 1761. In ms in CZ-K. See Brown (item 166).

72. *Don Juan, ou Le festin de pierre.* Ballet pantomime in three acts, scenario by Angiolini, Vienna: Trattnern, 1761.Vienna, Burgtheater, Oct. 17, 1761. G ii/1, ed. Richard Engländer, 1966; in ms in B-Bc, D-Bsb, D-Dlb, D-Mbs.

73. *La Citera assiedata.* Ballet pantomime in one act, scenario by Angiolini, after Favart (preface to *La Citera assiedata*, Vienna: van Ghelen, 1762). Vienna, Burgtheater, Sept. 15, 1762. Music lost. See Brown (item 166), and Croll (item 103).

74. *Les amours d'Alexandre et de Roxane (Alessandro).* Ballet pantomime in one act, scenario by Angiolini, missing. Vienna, Burgtheater, Oct. 4, 1764. G ii/2, forthcoming; in ms in A-Wn, B-Bc, CH-BEl, CZ-K, CZ-Pnm, D-Bsb, D-Dlb, D-DS, D-MÜu.

75. *Sémiramis.* Ballet pantomime in three acts, scenario by Angiolini, after Voltaire, Vienna: Trattnern, 1765. Vienna Burgtheater, Jan. 31, 1765. G ii/1; in ms in A-Wn, B-Bc, D-DS.

76. *Ifigenia in Aulide.* Ballet pantomime in one act, scenario by Angiolini, missing. Laxenburg, May 19, 1765. Music lost. See Croll (item 510).

77. *Achille in Sciro.* Ballet pantomime, scenario by Angiolini, missing. Composed for Innsbruck, summer 1765, not performed. In ms in CZ-K. See Brown (item 166), Hortschansky (item 179), and Gerber (item 522).

   New Grove (item 99) gives details of many more ballets probably by Gluck, the music for which is lost.

Instrumental Music

78. Trio Sonatas. Gv/1, ed. Friedrich-Heinrich Neumann, 1961 contains six trio sonatas for two violins and continuo, in C, G-minor, A, B-flat, E-flat, and F (London: Simpson, 1746); two trio sonatas for two violins and bass, in E, in ms in D-Bsb, and F, in ms in CZ-Pnm. *New Grove* (item 99) includes details of three further chamber works of doubtful ascription.

79. Sinfonias. Nine sinfonias in C, D, D, D, D, E, F, F, G are identifiable by incipits in Wotquenne (item 49). Of these, two have been published: No. 7 in F, ed. Hermann Scherchen, Mainz: Schott, nd; No. 9 in G, ed. A. Hoffmann, Wolfenbüttel: Möseler, 1950; ms copies of the remainder in A-Wgm, B-Bc,

CH-BEl, D-Bsb, D-Dlb, F-Pn, S-L, S-Skma. Twelve other sinfonias have been attributed to Gluck, some doubtful: sinfonias in D & F, ed. Rudolf Gerber, Kassel: Bärenreiter, 1953. See Gerber (item 522) and LaRue (item 523); ms copies of the remainder in A-Gd, CZ-Bm, CZ-Pnm, D-Dlb, D-Rtt, D-WRl, I-PAc, S-Skma.

2. A NOTE ON THE COLLECTED EDITIONS

Sämtliche Werke

The situation has changed radically since the first edition of this *Guide to Research*. The *Sämtliche Werke*, published by Bärenreiter, now extends to thirty volumes, planned to rise to thirty-five by the end of 2003, and contains the following works.

Orfeo ed Euridice, ed. Anna Amalie Abert & Ludwig Finscher, 1963, i/1

Telemaco, ed. Karl Geiringer,1972, i/2

Alceste (1767), ed. Gerhard Croll, 1988, i/3a (i/3b, commentary, planned for 2003)

Paride ed Elena, ed. Rudolf Gerber, 1954, i/4

Iphigénie en Aulide, ed. Marius Flothius, 1987, i/5a,b

Orphée et Eurydice, ed. Ludwig Finscher, 1967, i/6

Alceste (1776), ed. Rudolf Gerber, 1957, i/7

Armide, ed. Klaus Hortschansky, 1991, i/8

Iphigénie en Tauride, ed. Gerhard Croll, 1973, i/9

Écho et Narcisse, ed. Rudolf Gerber, 1953, i/10

Iphigenie auf Tauris, ed. Gerhard Croll, 1965, i/11

Don Juan and *Sémiramis*, ed. Richard Engländer, 1966, ii/1

Don Juan, Alessandro, Achille in Sciro, ii/2 (forthcoming in 2002)

Ipermestra, ed. Axel Beer, 1997, iii/6

Il re pastore, ed. Lázló Somfai, 1968, iii/8

La Semiramide riconosciuta, ed. Gerhard Croll and Thomas Hauschka, 1994, iii/12

Ezio (1750), ed. Gabriele Buschmeier, 1990, iii/14

La clemenza di Tito, ed. Franz Giegling, 1995, iii/16

Le cinesi, ed. Gerhard Croll, 1958, iii/17

La danza, ed. Gerhard Croll, 1969, iii/18

Antigono, iii/20 (planned for 2003)

Tetide, ed. Lázló Somfai, 1978, iii/22

Il trionfo di Clelia, iii/23 (planned for 2003)

Ezio (1763), ed. Gabriele Buschmeier, 1992, iii/24

Il Parnaso confuso, ed. Bernd Baselt, 1970, iii/25

La corona, ed. Gerhard Croll, 1974, iii/26

Le feste d'Apollo, iii/28a, b (planned for 2003)

L'île de Merlin, ed. Günter Hausswald, 1956, iv/1

Le diable à quatre, ed. Bruce Alan Brown, 1992, iv/3

L'ivrogne corrigé, ed. Franz Rühlmann, 1951, iv/5

Le cadi dupé, ed. Daniela Philippi, 1999, iv/6

La rencontre imprévue, ed. Harald Heckmann, 1964, iv/7

L'arbre enchanté (1775), iv/11 (forthcoming in 2002)

Trio Sonatas, ed. Friedrich-Heinrich Neumann, 1961, v/1

Die originalen Textbücher der bis 1990 in der Gluck-Gesamtausgabe er-schienenen Bühnenwerke, ed. Klaus Hortschansky, 1995, vii/1

A consequence of the already wide time span of production is that editorial approaches vary, reflecting changing aims and attitudes, but the series has on the whole succeeded in maintaining a good standard and usefully combines the function of producing scholarly editions with the provision of practical performing material. The introductory essays in conjunction with the critical textual commentaries provide a starting point for Gluck studies today.

Early Collected Editions

The earliest attempts at collected editions concentrated exclusively on the Paris operas. Hopkinson (item 43) argues that the sequence of eight full scores from Des Lauriers of Paris constitutes the first such attempt. Publication dates are uncertain and are inferred from the fact that Des Lauriers brought the plates from the Bureau d'Abonnement Musical, which went out of business in 1783, and, in the case of *Iphigénie en Tauride*, from the Bureau du Journal de Musique, which closed in 1779. The score of *Écho* is the first published edition.

Des Lauriers
  Armide, after 1783(?)

  Alceste, after 1783

  Iphigénie en Aulide, after 1783

  Iphigénie en Tauride, after 1779

  Orphée et Eurydice, after 1783

  Écho et Narcisse, 1779

  La Cythère assiégée, after 1783

  L'arbre enchanté, after 1783

Shortly after this, an edition of vocal scores was begun in Berlin, edited and published by Jean Charles Fréderic Rellstab. Four volumes were issued.

Rellstab
  Iphigénie en Tauride, 1788–1789

  Orphée et Eurydice, 1788–1789

  Alceste, 1796

  Armide, 1805–1806

The earliest French vocal scores followed in a collection called *Répertoire des opéras français,* edited by La Veuve Nicolo. Five volumes of Gluck's operas appeared as part of this series.

Veuve Nicolo
  Armide, 1823

  Iphigénie en Aulide, 1824

  Iphigénie en Tauride, 1824

  Alceste, 1824

  Orphée et Eurydice, 1824

Two attempts at critical editions, with investigative prefaces and textual commentaries, date from the close of the nineteenth century. The first was the much-respected Édition Pelletan; the first four volumes were published in Paris by Richault, the last two by Durand. The edition, in full score, comprises six volumes.

Édition Pelletan
  Iphigénie en Aulide, ed. Fanny Pelletan and B. Damcke, 1873

Iphigénie en Tauride, ed. Fanny Pelletan and B. Damcke, 1874

Alceste, ed. Fanny Pelletan and B. Damcke, 1874

Armide, ed. Fanny Pelletan, Camille Saint-Saëns, and Julien Tiersot, 1890

Orphée et Eurydice, ed. Fanny Pelletan, Camille Saint-Saëns, and Julien Tiersot, 1898

Écho et Narcisse, ed. Fanny Pelletan, Camille Saint-Saëns, and Julien Tiersot, 1902

Contemporaneously, a critical edition of vocal scores was published in Paris by Lemoine. The editor was F. A. Gevaert, and it offered the usual five operas.

Gevaert

Iphigénie en Aulide, 1899

Iphigénie en Tauride, 1900

Orphée et Eurydice, 1901

Armide, 1902

Alceste, 1902

Interest in a wider repertory resulted from the stimulus given to Gluck scholarship by the bicentenary celebrations. Two attempts at initiating a collected edition emanated from Leipzig. Max Arend, the leading Gluck scholar of the first decade of the century, began a new edition which succeeded in issuing no more than a single volume in full score: *Die Pilger von Mekka* (*La recontre imprévue*), ed. Arend, trans. Charlotte Rittberg. Leipzig: Verlag der Gluckgesellschaft, vol. 1, 1910. This was followed by Breitkopf & Härtel's Gluckgesellschaft, which ran to four volumes.

Gluckgesellschaft

Demofoonte, Act I in vocal score, ed. Julien Tiersot, 1914

Orpheus und Eurydike, vocal score, ed. Hans Kleemann, 1916

Klopstocks Oden und Lieder, ed. Gustav Beckmann, 1917

Sonaten 1–3, score and parts, ed. Gustav Beckmann, 1919, reprinted 1955

Single critical editions published in the Bavarian and Austrian Denkmäler should also be mentioned here, since they both constitute landmarks in scholarship and offer what could well be regarded as a series no more incomplete than most previous attempts at collected editions. All are in full score.

Denkmäler Editions

Le nozze d'Ercole e d'Ebe, ed. Hermann Abert, DTB, Bd 26, Jahrgang 14/2, Leipzig: Breitkopf & Härtel, 1914

Orfeo ed Euridice, ed. Hermann Abert, DTO, Bd 44a, Jahrgang 21,Vienna: Artaris, 1914

Don Juan, ed. Robert Haas, DTO, Bd. 60, Jahrgang 30, Vienna: Universal, Leipzig: Breitkopf & Härtel, 1923

L'innocenza giustificata, ed. Alfred Einstein, DTO Bd 82, Jahrgang 44, Vienna: Universal, 1937

Full bibliographical data is given in Hopkinson (item 43), which also lists many single editions of Gluck's published works. An extensive discussion of the editions available in 1958 appears in Boetticher (item 78).

3. AUTOGRAPH AND MANUSCRIPT HOLDINGS

Eighteenth-century manuscript copies of Gluck's works exist in abundance in libraries throughout Europe. A representative selection from these are mentioned above in the list of compositions. A number of works have never been published, for example *La contesa de'numi*, 1749, and some of these exist only in fragments, scattered between libraries, as is the case with *Demetrio*, 1742. Others can be reconstructed from a mixture of published numbers, self-borrowings, and single numbers in manuscript, for example *Artamene*, 1746.

The situation with autograph material is rather different. It is certain that the material is very limited. There are inevitable discrepancies between early records and the currently known tally. Among the most tantalizing losses is a version of "Io non chiedo" from *Alceste*, with a 48-bar coda that Gluck composed in order to turn the aria into a self-standing number for performance by Marianne Gluck (see *Allgemeine Musikalische Zeitung*, November 7, 1832, col. 746). Other fragments exist only in photocopies, for example those from *Iphigenie auf Tauris*, the originals of which were once housed in the Musikbibliothek Peters, Leipzig (see *Iphigenie auf Tauris*, G i/11). With the help of Daniela Philippi and the libraries concerned, I have been able to compile the following provisional and temporary list, with shelf-marks where known.

Autograph Scores and Fragments

Ipermestra (1744), CH-B (private collection): score of sinfonia

Artamene (1746), A-Wgm (A184, in Album Wimpffen I, 5): "Già presso al termine" (opening); "Se crudeli" (ending)

Ezio (1750), D-Bsb (Mus. ms. Gluck 3 c): "Ecco alle mie catene"

Issipile (1752), A-Wn(Mus. Hs. 41.405, A/Gluck 3): "Parto se vuoi così," previously in the possession of John Kallir, Scarsdale, New York

Orfeo ed Euridice (1762), A-Wn (MA. G. 1. E): "Trionfi amore", rejected sketch

Il trionfo di Clelia (1762), F-Po (Ms. Rés. 88): sinfonia (see *Orphée*)

Telemaco (1765), A-Wn (Ms. Hs. 18464, A/Gluck2): Act I scn1, bb. 180–253

Alceste (1767), GB-Lbl (Zweig. Ms. 34): "Misero! e che farò?"

Le feste d'Apollo (1769), A-Wgm (A 185): "Eccheggiar s'odano" (*Atto d'Aristeo*); US-Wc (Moldenhauer, Box 20) "Del figlio d'Apollo" (*Atto d'Aristeo*)

Orphée et Eurydice (1774), F-Po(Ms. Rés. 89): Act I, scns 1–4 (missing "L'espoir renaît"); Act II, scns 1–2 (missing scn 2, bb. 29–140); Act II, scn 3, bb. 1–55

S-Smf: Act II, scn 3, "O vous ombres"

F-Pn (Ms. 367): Act III, scn 1, bb. 1–157

F-Pn (Ms. 369): Act III, scn 1, bb. 158–184

D-Bsb (Mus. ms. autogr. Gluck 4): Act III, scn 1, bb. 308–326

US-STum (call-mark 375): Act III, scn 1, bb. 402–446

RUS-SPsc (No. 2, 64. 65): Act III, scn 3, sketch of ending of Chaconne

F-Po (Ms. Rés. 88): sinfonia to *Il trionfo di Clelia*, source for Act III, scn 3, "Air vif" & "Menuet"

L'arbre enchanté (1775), F-Pn (Ms. 366): autograph score, missing only third movement of Ouverture, & the air "Près de l'objet"

Alceste (1776), F-Pn (Rés. Vm² 150): complete score

CH-Bu (Geigy-Hagenbach 2636 Ms. 568): Act II, scn 1, "Air de danse" in G (doubtful)

D-Bsb (Mus. ms. autogr. Gluck 1): Act III, scn 1, fragment

Armide (1777), F-Pn (Ms. 370): Ouverture

F-Po (Rés. 87, 1–3): Act I; Act III, scns 1–2; Act IV

F-Pn (Ms. 368): Act V, scns 1–4

F-Pn (Ms. 371): Act V, last scene

Écho et Narcisse (1779), CH-CObodmer (Ms. 11655): Act III, beginning of final ballet

Iphigenie auf Tauris (1781), D-Bsb (Mus. ms. autogr. Gluck 2): Act IV, scns 4–7, fragment US-NYpm: sketch of vocal lines

II

General Background for the Study of Gluck

Primary Sources Dealing with the Reforms in Opera, Ballet, Acting, Singing, and Stage Design

1. Algarotti, Francesco. *Saggio sopra l'opera in musica*, 1754. 2nd ed., Livorno: Coltellini, 1763. 157 pp. ML3858 A37.

   Widely influential discussion on the contemporary theater. Deals with the choice of subject, the disadvantages of historical compared with mythological subject matter, the music, including the irrelevance of overtures, the tedium of *secco* recitative, the lack of dramatic truth in the arias, the excess of ornament; stage behavior, the irrelevance of dance episodes, and the inappropriateness of costume and scenery. Criticizes all aspects of the Italian theater, often commends the French traditions, and calls for "a thorough reform of all the constituent parts of Italian opera."

2. Angiolini, Gasparo. *Dissertation sur les ballets pantomimes des anciens pour servir de programme au ballet pantomime tragique de "Sémiramis"* . . . *le 31 janvier 1765*. Vienna: Trattnern, 1765. 55 pp., reprinted Milan: n.p., 1956. GV1787 A47.

   Criticizes ballet as a series of abstract patterns and acrobatic posturings. Attacks the succession of unlinked scenes and trivial spectacles, especially where the choreography has been devised to accompany preexisting music. Advocates a return to the pantomimic art of the Greeks and the Romans: "a declamation for the eyes."

3. ———. *Lettere di Gasparo Angiolini a Monsieur Noverre sopra i balli pantomimi*. Milan: Bianchi, 1773. 112 pp. ML3460 A2 A58.

   Restates his theory of the dance. Advocates that the story should be precisely interpreted by the movements of the dancers, and argues the importance of characterization through gesture. Refutes Noverre's claim (in item 31) to be the inventor of the *ballet d'action*, asserting the prior claim of Hilverding.

4. Arteaga, Esteban [Stefano]. *Le rivoluzioni del teatro musicale italiano dalla sua origine fino al presente*. Bologna: Trenti, 1783–1788. 3 vols. ML1733 3 A7; 2nd ed., Venice: Palese, 1785. 3 vols.

Influential and widely quoted source. Compares opera with spoken drama and concludes that its highest achievement is to move the emotions. In a brief historical survey, appreciates Metastasio's elegance but deplores his dependence on intrigue; condemns the ubiquity of the da capo, excessive ornamentation, the increasing size of orchestras, the metaphor aria, and the "ignorance and vanity of singers." Identifies Gluck as the most successful composer of the age who represents true emotions and draws realistic characters, but attacks Calzabigi's role in the reform, especially his replacement of dialogue with tableaux, claiming his reputation owed everything to Gluck's music (see Calzabigi, item 14).

5. Bachaumont, Louis Petit de, M. F. Pidansat de Mairobert, Moufle d'Angerville and others, eds. *Mémoires pour servir à l'histoire de la république des lettres en France depuis 1762 jusqu'à nos jours*. London: Adamson, 1777–1789. 36 vols. PQ273 B3.

Vols. 7–13 present a valuable eyewitness account of Paris in the 1770s. Although dealing only intermittently with the musical world, the journal covers both the premieres and the revised versions of Gluck's operas and their reception. See also Mairobert (item 339).

6. Beattie, James. "Essay on Poetry and Music as They Affect the Mind." *Essays*. Edinburgh: William Creech, and London: E. and C. Dilly, 2nd ed., 1778, pp. 1–317. PN1055 B4.

Lucid exposition of Enlightenment theory on opera: reinforces the Encyclopedists' advocacy of simplicity in word-setting, and deplores both the imitative excess of metaphor arias and superfluous ornamentation which weakens true expression.

7. Bérard, Jean-Antoine. *L'art du chant*. Paris: Dessaint, Prault, and Lambert, 1755. 158 pp. MT820 A2 B3. Facsimile reprint Geneva: Minkoff, 1972. MT820 B385 A7 1972.

Standard text on French singing. Detailed advice on tone production and pronunciation, expanding conventional orthography to give guidance on the pronunciation of mute e's and nasal consonants. Useful detail on the performance of ornaments, for some of which Bérard invents new signs.

8. Brown, John. *A Dissertation on the Rise, Union and Power, the Progressions, Separations and Corruptions of Poetry and Music.* London: Davis, 1763. 246 pp. ML3849 B87. Facsimile reprint New York: Garland, 1971. ML3849 B87 1763a.

Widely read and influential discussion of the relationship between poetry and music. Looks back to a golden age when poet and musician were one; deplores modern word-setting as inexpressive and unnatural; criticizes contemporary performance practice, including excessive ornamentation, encores, and the use of castratos.

9. Burney, Charles. *The Present State of Music in France and Italy.* London, 1771, 2nd ed., 1773; many reprints, including *Music, Men and Manners in France and Italy, 1770: Being the Journal Written by Charles Burney during a Tour through those Countries Undertaken to Collect Material for a General History of Music.* London: Folio Society, 1969. xxix, 245 pp. ISBN 85067 020 9. ML195 B961.

Essential background to personalities, performances, and aesthetic arguments.

10. ———. *The Present State of Music in Germany, the Netherlands and United Provinces.* London: 1775, reprinted New York: Broude, 1969. 2 vols. ML195 B963.

Extensive description of Burney's encounters with Gluck. Eyewitness accounts of many of his contemporaries, including Guadagni and Metastasio.

11. ———. *A General History of Music, from the Earliest Times to the Present Period.* London: Printed for the Author, 1786–1789. Ed. Frank Mercer, New York: Dover Publications, 1957. 4 vols in 2. ML159 B96 1957.

Indispensable background to the period: a contemporary's view of the eighteenth-century musical scene. Includes further accounts of meetings with Gluck and the reception of his operas in London.

12. Calzabigi, Ranieri de'. "Dissertazione di Ranieri de'Calsabigi, dell'Accademia di Cortona, su le poesie drammatiche del Signor Abate Pietro Metastasio." *Poesie del Signor Abate Pietro Metastasio.* Paris: La Vedova Quillau, 1755, vol. 1, pp. xix–cciv. PQ4717 A17.

Major document for the reform of the libretto. Evidence of the warm esteem in which Calzabigi, like Gluck, originally held Metastasio; shows a detailed knowledge of *tragédie lyrique*, but appears ambivalent towards its aims. Advocates a simpler, more declamatory setting of librettos with fewer closed forms than in Metastasian opera.

13. ———— (?). *Lettre sur le méchanisme de l'opéra italien.* Naples, Paris: Duchesne and Lambert, 1756. xiv, 122 pp.

Attributed to Calzabigi by Heartz (in item 118); see also Brown (item 166). Claims to be inspired by Calzabigi's "Dissertazione" (item 12). Pithy and trenchant criticism of contemporary opera; praises pathetic arias, *obbligato* recitative, and the duet from Italian opera, and the chorus and dramatic continuity from French opera. Proposes a fusion of the two national traditions.

14. ————. *Risposta . . . alla critica ragionalissima della poesie drammatiche del R. de'Calsabigi, fatta da baccelliere D. Stefana Arteaga.* Venice: Curti, 1790. 224 pp. ML429 C14 A8.

Refutes Arteaga's criticism in item 4. Calzabigi asserts the importance of his own role in Gluck's reform and attacks Metastasio's dramatic system. Discussed by Einstein in item 545.

15. Corri, Domenico. *The Singer's Preceptor.* London: Chappell, 1810, reprinted 1811. 84 pp. MT830 C6.

A practical singing tutor. Corri, a pupil of Porpora, provides wide-ranging insights into performance practice of the second half of the eighteenth century. Deals with ornamentation, *rubato*, and the dramatic interpretation of a variety of styles. See also item 303.

16. Cramer, Carl Friedrich. *Magazin der Musik.* Hamburg: Der Musikalischen Niederlage, 1783–1786. 4 vols. ML4 M2.

Useful primary source for musical life over a wide area of Europe. Includes reviews and reports of new music, lists of instrumentalists and singers, occasional opera librettos, and many anecdotes. Intermittent references to Gluck throughout. Unreliable index to first two volumes only.

17. Diderot, Denis. "De la poésie dramatique." *Collection complette des œuvres philosophiques, littéraires et dramatiques de M. Diderot.* London, 1773, vol. 5, pp. i–cxii, reprinted in *Diderot's Writings on the Theatre*, ed. F. C. Green. Cambridge: Cambridge University Press, 1936. 317 pp. PQ1979 A6 G7.

Detailed criticism of mid-eighteenth-century French theater. Although principally concerned with spoken drama, also analyzes stage design and costume. Advocates truth, simplicity, and verisimilitude to enhance the representation of the drama.

18. ————. *Paradoxe sur le comédien.* Paris, 1830. Included in Green's edition of Diderot (item 17) and in a critical edition by Ernest Dupuy, Paris: Société

Française d'Imprimerie, 1902. xxxxiv, 178 pp. Trans. Walter Herries Pollock as *The Paradox of Acting*, with a preface by Henry Irving. London: Chatto & Windus, 1883. xx, 108 pp. PN2061 D5.

Written in 1773, provides valuable background to the reform of acting styles and the new attitude to expression on the stage. Argues the superiority of technique over "sensibility" both for the actor and the poet. Garrick's seminal role in the reform of acting acknowledged.

19. Dubos, Jean-Baptiste, Abbé. *Réflexions critiques sur la poësie et la peinture* (1719). 4th ed., Paris: Mariette, 1740. 3 vols. N63 D8.

   In the course of a treatise on aesthetics, makes many valuable observations about the stage, especially the part played by costume and gesture in the mimetic arts.

20. Du Roullet, François-Louis Gand Leblanc. *Lettre sur les drames-opéra*. Amsterdam and Paris: Esprit, 1776, reprinted in Lesure (item 336), vol. 2, pp. 109–161.

   States the reforms Du Roullet introduced into the libretto of *Iphigénie en Aulide*, emphasizing where he departs from Quinault's practice. Claims responsibility for the structure of the scenes and for the provision of verse in appropriate meters related to the emotions of the character; see, however, Buschmeier (item 423), who argues that Gluck ignored some of the structures devised by Du Roullet. See also Angermüller (item 541).

21. Gottsched, Johann Christoph. *Versuch einer critischen Dichtkunst*. Leipzig: Breitkopf, 1730. 4th ed., 1751.1st ed. reprinted Darmstadt: Wissenschaftliche Buchgesellschaft, 1977. xxxii, 808 pp. ISBN 3 534 01328 X. PN1031 G63 1977.

   Argues for a need to reform German dramatic poetry by establishing neoclassical tastes and techniques. Advocates realism and nature in language and subject matter. Condemns opera seria on the grounds that it lacks dramatic truth, outrages reason, and lacks precedents in the classical age. Gottsched's importance as background to the reform of opera lies chiefly in the numerous responses, almost all adversely critical, that he provoked in eighteenth-century aesthetic literature. See, for example, Mattheson (item 28).

22. Grimm, Friedrich Melchior. *Le petit prophète de Boehmisch-Broda*. Paris, 1744. 2nd ed., 1753. 56 pp. ML1727 33 G8. Trans. Oliver Strunk as "The little prophet of Boemischbroda" in *Source Readings in Music History*. New York: Norton, 1950, pp. 619–635. ML160 S89.

Satirical fantasy giving the flavor of the aesthetic debates forming the Querelle des Bouffons in mid-eighteenth-century Paris. Attacks all aspects of *tragédie lyrique*.

23. Kelly, Michael. *Reminiscences*. London: Colburn, 1826. 2 vols, reprinted New York: Da Capo Press, 1968. ML420 K292.

 Attractive primary source for eighteenth-century theatrical background. Includes eyewitness account of Gluck (vol. 1, pp. 254–256), the source for Gluck's tribute to Handel. Probably not written by Kelly but assembled from his conversations by his friend Theodore Hook.

24. Khevenhüller-Metsch, Johann Josef. *Aus der Zeit Maria Theresias. Tagebuch*, ed. Rudolf Khevenhüller-Metsch and Hans Schlitter. Vienna: Holzhausen, 1907–1925. 7 vols. DB73 K4 A2.

 Provides valuable evidence of the daily activities of the imperial family and in particular their attendance at operatic performances. See also Grossegger (item 322).

25. Mancini, Giambattista. *Pensieri, e riflessioni pratiche sopra il canto figurato* (1774); enlarged in 3rd ed., as *Riflessioni pratiche sul canto figurato*, Milan: Galeazzi, 1777, partly reprinted in Andrea della Corte, ed., *Canto e bel canto*. Turin: Paravia, 1923. 274 pp. MT823 C67.

 Singing tutor, developing Tosi's method (in item 37); gives practical guidance on singing technique and performance practice. Nevertheless, in his appendix, "Vicende degli stili del canto di Gluck al novecento," della Corte argues the limitations of using pedagogic material as evidence of performing conventions and analyzes Gluck's style as demanding a new, naturalistic delivery far removed from the style taught by Mancini, despite the latter's warm advocacy of Gluck's genius.

26. Manfredini, Vincenzo. *Difesa della musica moderna e de' suoi celebri esecutori*. Bologna: Trenti, 1788. 208 pp. ML290 3 M27. Trans. Patricia Howard as *In Defence of Modern Music*. New York: Mellen Press, 2002. xxxix, 166 pp. ISBN 0 7734 7087 5. ML1733.3 M46 2002.

 Though far from unappreciative of Gluck's operas, Manfredini defends the unreformed Italian genre of opera seria and its development in the last quarter of the eighteenth century. A useful counterpoise to the heated polemic of the reform.

27. Marcello, Benedetto. *Il teatro alla moda*. c. 1720. 2nd ed., Venice: Borghi di Belisania, 1720 or 1721. 72 pp. ML65 M25. Many reprints. Trans. with an

introductory essay by Reinhard G. Pauly, "Benedetto Marcello's Satire on Early 18th-century Opera," appeared in *The Musical Quarterly* 34 (1948): 222–233, 371–403; 35 (1949): 85–105. ISSN 0027 4631. ML1 M725.

Widely discussed satire on opera seria, attacking librettists, composers, and above all singers for the abuses of Italian opera. Pauly's essay traces the history of the various editions and mentions other eighteenth-century satires on opera. But see Kretzschmar (item 329).

28. Mattheson, Johann. *Die neueste Untersuchung der Singspiele*. Hamburg: Christian Herold, 1774. 168 pp. ML3858 M41.

Defends mid-eighteenth-century opera against Gottsched's attack (in item 21). Distinguishing between "Wahr und wahrscheinlich," argues that verisimilitude should not be confused with truth; explains the role of convention in opera in creating an imitation of nature which can never be identical with it.

29. Michelessi, Domenico. *Memorie intorno alla vita ed agli scritti del Conte Francesco Algarotti*. Venice: Pasquali, 1770. 205 pp. DG545 8 A5 M5.

Portrays Algarotti (item 1) as a widely cultured writer, in touch with the most influential thinkers of his age. Argues that although Algarotti's essay on the reform of opera forms an insignificant part of his writings, it nevertheless shows the application of a keen rationalist mind to the irrational conventions of opera.

30. Milizia, Francesco. *Trattato completo, formale e materiale del teatro*. Venice: Pasquali, 1794. 104 pp. PN1654 M5 1794.

A highly critical account of opera in Italy at the end of the eighteenth century, describing a genre untouched by Gluck's reforms (compare Manfredini, item 26). Deplores overtures unconnected to operas, arias with overlong introductory ritornellos, intrusive accompaniments, *passaggi*, and excessive repetition. Useful comments on stage scenery and production practices, including (pp. 77–80) descriptions of eighteen European theaters with dimensions and structure.

31. Noverre, Jean-Georges. *Lettres sur la danse et sur les ballets*. Lyons: Delaroche, 1760. 484 pp. ML3460 A2 N94.

Detailed exposition of the arguments in favor of verisimilitude in poetry, painting, and dance; advocates realism in gesture, costume, and design. Attacks "geometric" choreography and overconcern with symmetry and abstract pattern; suggests instead a combination of gesture and mime to enrich traditional dance steps and an understanding of the human body to promote a natural use of the limbs. Discusses the relationship of dance to music and the role of ballet in opera.

32. ———. *Lettres sur la danse, sur les ballets et les arts.* St. Petersburg: n.p., 1803–1804. ML3460 N95 1803. 2nd ed., *Lettres sur les arts imitateurs en général, et sur la danse en particulier.* Paris: Collin, 1807. 2 vols.

Continues the argument of item 31. Much material repeated, though Noverre withdraws his earlier opinion that ballet can recreate classical drama, here contending that the Greco-Roman theater was based on mime rather than dance.

33. Planelli, Antonio. *Dell'opere in musica.* Naples: Donato Campo, 1772. 272 pp. ML3858 A2 P7.

Essay on taste in Italian opera of the second half of the century. Reflects the ideas of Algarotti (item 1), Noverre (items 31 and 32), and the Encyclopedists (in Oliver, item 344). Cites *Alceste* as a model of music drama. Important discussion of eighteenth-century production methods—acting, dance, costume, and design—in which the key terms of the reform, "nature," "truth," and "verisimilitude" recur.

34. Rousseau, Jean-Jacques. *Lettre sur la musique française.* Paris 1753. 92 pp. ML1727 33 R7.

Influential contribution to the Querelle des Bouffons. Attacks all aspects of French opera, including the suitability of the French language for musical setting; argues that Italian opera has all the musical and dramatic advantages.

35. ———. *Dictionnaire de musique.* Paris: Veuve Duchesne, 1768. 547 pp., reprinted Paris: Art et Culture, 1977. 2 vols. ML108 R8 1977.

Incorporates Rousseau's articles for the *Encyclopédie*, with some revision. Entries under Opéra, Récitatif, Air, Accent, and Harmonie furnish a valuable account of Encyclopedist attitudes to changes in French music in the mid-eighteenth century. Attacks French *tragédie lyrique* and is strongly supportive of Italian opera.

36. Scheibe, Johann Adolph. *Critischer Musicus.* Hamburg: Thomas von Wierings Erben, 1738–1740. 2 vols. 2nd ed., Leipzig: Breitkopf, 1745. 1059 pp. ML4 C8.

Panoramic survey of mid-eighteenth-century music in a collection of articles written between 1737 and 1740, dealing with topics of current interest and controversy. Critical of early opera seria in Germany and urges a simplification of drama along Metastasian lines; argues that the overture should prepare the listener for the subsequent drama, though Scheibe does not envisage Gluck's organic integration of overture and scene.

37. Tosi, Pierfrancesco. *Opinioni de cantori antichi e moderni*. Bologna, 1723. Ed. Luigi Leonesi, Naples: Gennaro & Morano, 1904, also in Andrea della Corte, ed., *Canto e bel canto*. Turin: Paravia, 1923. 274 pp. MT823 C67.

   Seminal singing tutor for the eighteenth century, method in which all Gluck's Italian singers were trained. Gives specific instructions for the performance of ornamentation, *rubato,* and the expressive delivery of recitative and aria. Compare Mancini (item 25).

III

Sources and Resources for Gluck Research

1. BIBLIOGRAPHIES AND THEMATIC CATALOGUES

38. Arend, Max. "Ergänzungen und Berichtigungen zu Wotquennes thematischem Verzeichnis der Gluck'schen Werke." *Die Musik* 1913, reprinted in *Zur Kunst Glucks* (item 80), pp. 173–184.

    Supplies small amendments to Wotquenne (item 49), identifying the March in Wotquenne, p. 162, as belonging to *Demofoonte*; establishes the location of the libretto of *La danza* and the manuscript score of the Seventh Trio Sonata.

39. Eitner, Robert. *Biographisch-bibliographisches Quellen-Lexikon der Musiker und Musikgelehrten der christlichen Zeitrechnung bis zur Mitte des neunzehnten Jahrhunderts.* Leizpig: Breitkopf & Härtel, 1900–1904, reprinted Graz: Akadamische Druck und Verlagsanstalt, 1959–1960, vol. 4, pp. 281–288. ML105 E37.

    Contains brief outline biography of Gluck supported by detailed bibliographical references, followed by general bibliography of books and periodicals and a work list with library sources of first editions and some manuscripts. Some inaccuracies and spurious works included, but a valuable starting point for research.

40. Fétis, François-Joseph. *Biographie universelle des musiciens et bibliographie général de la musique* (1835–1844). 2nd ed., Paris: Didot Frères, 1860–1866, vol. 4, pp. 28–40. *Supplément*, ed. Arthur Pougin, 1878–1880, vol. 1, pp. 391–394. ML105 F42.

A biographical account based on Schmid (item 144); includes work list and bibliography with some annotations. The supplement contains an extensive annotated bibliography of primary sources dealing with the Gluck-Piccinni rivalry, complied by Thoinan.

41. Forkel, Johann Nicolaus. "Streitigkeiten über Vorzüge der italienischen und französischen Musik, über die Bouffonisten in Paris, über Rousseaus Beurtheilung der französischen Musik, und über die theatralische Musik des Ritter Gluck." *Allgemeine Literatur der Musik.* Leipzig: Schwickertschen Verlag, 1792, pp. 176–183, reprinted Hildesheim: Olms, 1962. ML105 F73.

Bibliography of topics mentioned in the title; some items briefly annotated.

42. Fuchs, Aloys. "Thematisches Verzeichnis sämtlicher Compositionen des K.K. Hof-Componisten Christoph Ritter con Gluck." *Neue Berliner Musikzeitung* 5/27 (1851): 207–210. ML5 N2.

A number of Fuch's early attempts to compile a complete thematic catalogue exist in ms in D-Bsb, mss 575, 577. This published work contains a list of forty works by Gluck (twenty-two with incipits of overtures), with dates of composition, first performances, and sources. Also identifies sixteen Gluck portraits and six busts. While obviously superseded by Wotquenne (item 49), it provides evidence of the state of Gluck research in mid-nineteenth-century Germany.

43. Hopkinson, Cecil. *A Bibliography of the Printed works of C. W. von Gluck 1714–1787.* London, 1959. 2nd ed., New York: Broude, 1967. xiv, 96 pp. ML134 G58 H7.

Useful attempt to update Wotquenne's information on early published scores, giving accurate library locations of rare copies. Much information on later publications of both full and vocal scores. Includes some vocal items not in Wotquenne. Lists published librettos and includes extensive bibliography. Essential to consult reviews of 1st ed. (item 46) and 2nd ed. (item 45) for factual corrections.

44. Keller, Otto. "Gluck-Bibliographie." *Die Musik* (item 88): 23–37, 85–91. ML5 M9.

Covers books and periodicals; divided into general topics, Gluck and his contemporaries, aesthetics, and discussions of individual works. Many items do not appear in later bibliographies. Potentially a useful source but to be used with great caution: not all bibliographical references are sufficiently complete for the items to be traceable and some entries are misleading, being merely cross-references to lists of publications; many items of ephemeral interest only.

45. Lesure, François. "Cecil Hopkinson: 'A Bibliography of the Printed Works of C. W. von Gluck 1714–1787.'" *Revue de musicologie* 43 (1967): 195. ML5 R32.

   Brief review of 2nd ed. of Hopkinson (item 43). Corrects the dating of the Des Lauriers editions of *Armide* and *Iphigénie en Tauride* and the *Ezio* fragment published by De la Chevardière.

46. Neumann, Friedrich-Heinrich. "Cecil Hopkinson: 'A Bibliography of the Printed Works of C. W. von Gluck 1714–1787.'" *Die Musikforschung* 13 (1960): 227–230. ISSN 0027 4801. ML5 M9437.

   Reviews the 1st ed. of Hopkinson (item 43). Includes an extensive list of amendments, which are incorporated in the 2nd ed.

47. Surian, Elvidio. *A Checklist of Writings on 18th-Century French and Italian Opera (Excluding Mozart)*. Hackensack, NJ: Joseph Boonin, 1970. xiv, 121 pp. ML128 04 S9.

   Wide-ranging bibliography, organized to include eighteenth-century and modern writings on opera (by country, city, and individual composers), librettos and librettists, singers and singing, and theatrical production.

48. Wortsmann, Stephan. *Die deutsche Gluck-Literatur*. Nürnberg: Koch, 1914. viii, 121 pp. ML410 G51 W68.

   Much more than a bibliography: the most important survey of Gluck studies in the German language up to 1914. Critically analyzes earlier bibliographies, dictionary entries, biographies, general and specialized studies, and studies of Gluck in comparison with other composers. Sifts conflicting accounts and is useful in tracing erroneous anecdotes to their sources.

49. Wotquenne, Alfred. *Catalogue thématique des oeuvres de Chr. W. v. Gluck*. Leipzig: Breitkopf & Härtel, 1904. Trans. Josef Liebeskind as *Chr. W. v. Gluck: Thematisches Verzeichnis seiner Werke*. Breitkopf & Härtel, 1904. *Ergänzungen und Nachträger / Compléments et Suppléments* by Josef Liebeskind (parallel text), Leipzig: Gebrüder Reinecke, 1911. 20 pp., reprinted Hildesheim: Olms, 1967. xi, 246 pp. ML134 G56 W6 1967.

   Urgently in need of total revision. Omissions and corrections have been noted by generations of scholars (earliest review by Max Arend, item 38). Nevertheless an essential source when used in combination with Hopkinson (item 43) and the critical commentaries to the *Sämtliche Werke*.

50. Wurzbach, Constantin. "Christoph Willibald Ritter von Gluck." *Biographisches Lexikon des Kaisertums Österreich enthaltend die Lebenskizzen der denkwürdigen Personen welche 1750 bis 1850 im Kaiserstaate . . . gelebt haben.* Vienna, 1856–1891, reprinted New York: Johnson, 1966, vol. 2, pp. 221–232. CT903 W81.

Short biography and detailed bibliography of Gluck literature, chiefly in Austrian sources. Includes many items not listed in other bibliographies.

2. LETTERS

51. Alcari, Cesare. "La cartella no. 88." *Musica d'oggi* 14/10 (1932): 257–260. ML5 M721.

Discusses letters, dated January to March 1770, between Gluck and Gasparo Caroli concerning the employment of the Bolognese singer Gabriella Tagliaferri. Four letters from Gluck, dated January 26, February 22, and March 1 and 19 are published in full.

52. Cauchie, Maurice. "Gluck et ses éditeurs parisiens." *Le ménestrel* 28 (1927): 309–311. ML5 M465.

Commentary on the Kruthoffer letters in Kinsky (item 59), Komorn (item 60) and Pereyra (item 63), relating to the publication of *Iphigénie en Aulide* and *La Cythère assiégée.*

53. Hammelmann, Hans and Michael Rose. "New Light on Calzabigi and Gluck." *The Musical Times* 110 (1969): 609–611. ISSN 0027 4666. ML5 M85.

Gives the first English translation of a letter from Calzabigi to Prince Kaunitz, dated March 6, 1767, on the subject of the *Alceste* premiere. Calzabigi shows himself to be a practical man of the theater, attributing *Orfeo*'s success to Guadagni's creation of the title role and giving full credit to Gluck's genius. The tone is notably different from Calzabigi's later claims to have played the major role in the reform.

54. Hortschansky, Klaus. "Christoph Willibald Gluck: The Collected Correspondence and Papers." *Die Musikforschung* 17 (1965): 469–471. ISSN 0027 4801. ML5 M9437.

Systematically corrects errors and omissions in Mueller von Asow (item 61). Includes a list of published letters ignored by von Asow.

55. ———. "Glucks Sendungsebewusstsein. Dargestellt an einem unbekannten Gluck-Brief." *Die Musikforschung* 21 (1968): 30–35. ISSN 0027 4801. ML5 M9437.

Discusses Gluck's letter to Padre Martini dated July 14, 1770, in which Gluck sought Martini's help in obtaining performances of his reform operas outside Vienna. Notes that several key phrases associated with the aims of the reform appear in this letter. Full text of letter is given in Italian and German.

56. Howard, Patricia. *Gluck: An Eighteenth-Century Portrait in Letters and Documents*. Oxford: Clarendon Press, 1995. xv, 271 pp. ISBN 0 19 816385 1. ML410 G5 H688 1995.

The most complete collection of letters and documents in English translation currently available. Corrects errors and fills in gaps in Mueller von Asow (item 61); many items published for the first time in English.

57. ———. "Gluck the Family Man: An Unpublished Letter." *Music & Letters* 77/1 (1996): 92–96. ISSN 0027 4224. ML5 M64.

Examines the text of a hitherto unpublished letter from Gluck to his brother-in-law which reveals a number of characteristic attitudes. The letter is given in facsimile, transcript, and translation.

58. Kaplan, James Maurice. "Eine Ergänzung zu Glucks Korrespondenz." Trans. G. Nobel and J. Neur. *Die Musikforschung* 31 (1978): 314–317. ISSN 0027 4801. ML5 M9437.

Deals with an event during Gluck's last year in Paris, when the soprano Dupuis replaced Levasseur in the title role of *Iphigénie en Tauride*. Gives the text of Gluck's letter to the *Journal de Paris*, disclaiming that he had personally chosen and trained Dupuis, a review of the performance, and a letter from Dupuis to Gluck, protesting at her dismissal.

59. Kinsky, Georg. *Glucks Briefe an Franz Kruthoffer*. Vienna-Prague-Leipzig: Strache Verlag, 1927. 79 pp. ML420 G5.

Gives the text of forty-five letters from Gluck to Kruthoffer between April 15, 1775 and August 4, 1783. Full and accurate annotations.

60. Komorn, Maria. "Ein ungedruckter Brief Glucks." *Neue Zeitschrift für Musik* 99 (1932): 672–675. ML5 N4.

Gives the text of a letter dated November 29, 1776 from Gluck to Kruthoffer, hitherto missing from the Gluck-Kruthoffer sequence. The letter proves that Gluck had left Paris in June 1776 to spend the remainder of the year in Vienna.

61. Mueller von Asow, Erich Hermann, and Hedwig Mueller von Asow, eds. *The Collected Correspondence and Papers of Christoph Willibald Gluck.* Trans. Stewart Thomson. London: Barrie & Rockliff, 1962. xi, 239 pp. ML410 G5 A413.

   For many years the most complete edition of the letters in English. Many inaccuracies and omissions; reviewed in Hortschansky (item 54); superseded by Howard (item 56).

62. Nohl, Ludwig. *Musiker-Briefe. Eine Sammlung Briefe von C. W. von Gluck, Ph. E. Bach, J. Haydn, C. M. von Weber und F. Mendelssohn-Bartholdy.* Leipzig: Duncker & Humblot, 1867. x, 354 pp. ML90 N74 1867.

   Includes the prefaces to *Alceste* and *Paride ed Elena*, fourteen letters from Gluck's Paris period, and his will.

63. Pereyra, Marie Louise. "Vier Gluck-Briefe." *Die Musik* (item 88): 10–15.

   Contains the text of four letters to Kruthoffer.

64. Prod'homme, Jacques-Gabriel. "Gluck." *Écrits des musiciens.* Paris: Mercure de France. 1912, pp. 374–437. ML90 P9.

   Brief biographical introduction followed by twenty-six letters, including the prefaces and dedications to *Alceste, Paride ed Elena, Iphigénie en Aulide, Orphée et Eurydice,* and *Iphigénie en Tauride.* All material in French.

65. ———. "Letters de Gluck et à propos de Gluck (1776–1787)." *Zeitschrift der Internationalen Musikgesellschaft* 13/8 (1912): 257–265. ML5 I68.

   Contains the text of seven previously unpublished letters from Gluck; in addition, a letter from Salieri concerning Gluck's death, dated December 5, 1787, and one from Piccinni, dated December 13, 1787, proposing the foundation of an annual concert in Gluck's honour. See Winternitz (item 366).

66. R., L. "Correspondance inédite de Gluck." *La revue musicale* (item 89): 1–16. ML5 R613.

   Gives the text of sixteen previously unpublished letters.

67. Spulak, Roswitha. "Ein unbekanntes Schriftstück Christoph Willibald Glucks." *Die Musikforschung* 40 (1987): 345–349. ISSN 0027 4801. ML5 M9437.

The earliest extant letter in Gluck's hand; notes the correspondence between Gluck and Franz and Marianne Pirker in 1748, in which Gluck gave various commissions to the Pirkers, including an order for a watch. Reproduces text and facsimile.

*Tenschert, Roland. "Documente des Lebens." *Christoph Willibald Gluck. Der grosse Reformator der Oper.* Cited below as item 150.

68. Tiersot, Julien. "Pour la centenaire de Gluck: lettres et documents inédits." *Le ménestrel* 23–35 (1914): 214–215, 221–222, 236–237, 243–245, 261–262, 266–267, 270–271. ML5 M465.

Substantial collection of previously unpublished letters and documents in F-Pn dating from Gluck's arrival in Paris in 1774, with commentary. (The sequence is unfinished owing to the outbreak of war.)

69. Unger, Max. "Zur Entstehungsgeschichte des *Trionfo di Clelia* von Gluck." *Neue Zeitschrift für Musik* 82 (1915): 269–275. ML5 N4.

Letters from Luigi Bevilacqua of Bologna to Lodovico Preti in Vienna concerning the engagement of Gluck to compose an opera for the reopening of the public opera house in Bologna. The aria "Ah celar la bella face" is printed between pp. 280–281.

3. ICONOGRAPHY

70. Leroux, Jean. "L'iconographie du chevalier Gluck." *La revue musicale* (item 89): 39–47. ML5 R613.

Illustrated discussion of the portraits by Duplessis, Greuze, and Houdon.

71. Prod'homme, Jacques-Gabriel. "Les portraits français de Gluck." *Rivista musicale italiana* 25 (1918): 29–62. ML5 R66.

A critical discussion, with illustrations, of the portraits by Duplessis, Greuze, Houdon, Françin, and Corbet.

72. Tenschert, Roland. *Christoph Willibald Gluck. Sein Leben in Bildern.* Leipzig: Bibliographisches Institut, 1938. 40 pp., plus 57 plates. ML410 G5 T3.

Major iconographical study: reproduces a collection of portraits of Gluck and his contemporaries, scenes of activity, title pages, etc.

73. Van der Borren, C. "Un portrait inédit de Gluck par Duplessis." *Revue de musicologie* 4 (1925): 105–106. Ml5 R32.

Describes a newly discovered pastel attributed to Duplessis, a version of the well-known Duplessis oil.

74. Vogel, Emil. "Gluck-Portraits." *Jahrbuch der Musikbibliothek Peters* 4 (1897): 11–18. ML5 J15.

A critical account of all known Gluck portraits.

4. SURVEYS OF RESEARCH

75. Abert, Anna Amalie. "Die Oper zwischen Barock und Romantik." *Acta musicologica* 40 (1977): 137–193. ISSN 0001 6241. ML5 I6.

An overview of research since the war. Useful annotated bibliographies of various national opera schools. The entry for Gluck is extensive: pp. 175–182.

76. Abert, Hermann. "Zum Geleit." *Gluck-Jahrbuch* 1 (item 87): 1–8.

Introduction to the first *Gluck-Jahrbuch*, identifying gaps in Gluck research. Deals with Gluck's relevance in the twentieth century and the relationship of his dramatic concepts to those of Wagner. Sets out the aim of the series.

77. Becker, Heinz. "Zur Situation der Opernforschung." *Die Musikforschung* 27/2 (1974): 153–165. ISSN 0027 4801. ML5 M9437.

Argues that the chief aim of opera research should be to promote the performances of works which were historically significant in their own day. Suggests that a study of Gluck's operas is incomplete unless it embraces a study of the operas of Piccinni.

78. Boetticher, Wolfgang. "Über Entwicklung und gegenwärtigen Stand der Gluck-Edition." *Acta musicologica* 30 (1958): 99–112. ISSN 0001 6241. ML5 I6.

Reports on the progress towards a collected edition of Gluck's works. Reviews previous attempts to compile such an edition, and lists all major twentieth-century editions. The footnotes constitute an extensive and valuable bibliography.

79. Croll, Gerhard. "Gluckforschung und Gluck-Gesamtausgabe." *Musik und Verlag. Karl Vötterle zum 65. Geburtstag am 12 April 1968*, ed. Richard Baum and Wolfgang Rehm. Kassel: Bärenreiter, 1968, pp. 192–196. ML55 V537 M9.

Retrospective view of Gluck research with special reference to its debt to Johann Friedrich Reichardt, Alfred Wotquenne, Hermann Abert, and Rudolf Gerber. Outlines the particular problems involved in dealing with the source material for Gluck's ballets and sinfonias.

5. COLLECTIONS OF ESSAYS AND CONFERENCE ACTS

80. Arend, Max. *Zur Kunst Glucks*. Regensburg: Bosse, 1914. 247 pp. ML140 G5 A7.

   A collection of essays and reviews of varying importance but all evincing Arend's acute perception and warm advocacy of Gluck. Although many of the contents are designedly ephemeral, the collection gives a useful overview of Gluck's work in the theater in the first decade of the twentieth century. Many essays cited separately.

81. Croll, Gerhard, and Monica Woitas, eds. *Gluck in Wien (Gluck-Studien 1)*. Kassel: Bärenreiter, 1989. 188 pp. ISBN 3 7618 0929 8. ML410 G5 K6 1989.

   Papers from an international conference on Gluck in Vienna, November 1987; most cited separately.

82. Del Monte, Claudio and Vincenzo Raffaele Segreto, eds. *Christoph Willibald Gluck nel 200° anniversario della morte*. Parma: Editrice Grafice STEP Cooperativa, 1987. ML410 G5 C38 1987.

   Collection of forty-eight essays, mostly addressed to the general reader, covering many aspects of Gluck's life and works; some cited separately.

83. Hortschansky, Klaus, ed. *Christoph Willibald Gluck und die Opernreform (Wege der Forschung, vol. 613)*. Darmstadt: Wissenschaftliche Buchgesellschaft, 1989. 435 pp. ISBN 3 534 08666 X.

   Collection of essays on Gluck, many of them published previously; most cited separately.

84. Vetter, Walther. *Mythos-Melos-Musica*. Leipzig: Deutscher Verlag für Musik, 1957, 1961. 2 vols. ML60 V44.

   Collection of essays, many dealing with Gluck and his contemporaries; most cited separately.

6. YEARBOOKS AND SPECIAL ISSUES OF PERIODICALS

85. *L'Avant Scène Opéra.*

Three issues devoted to Gluck operas, each containing historical and analytical essays, images of past productions, and complete librettos.

No. 62 (1984), 138 pp. *Iphigénie en Tauride.* ISSN 0764 2873

No. 73 (1985), 130 pp. *Alceste.* ISSN 0395 0670

No. 192 (1999), 138 pp. *Orphée.* ISSN 0764 2873

86. *Chigiana* nuova serie 9–10 (1972–1973): 235–592. ML5 C38.

Special Gluck issue. Contains papers from an international conference on "Gluck e la cultura italiana nella Vienna del suo tempo." Accademia Musicale Chigiana in collaboration with the University of Siena, September 1973; most of the contents are cited separately.

87. *Gluck-Jahrbuch,* ed. Hermann Abert. Leipzig: Breitkopf & Härtel, 1914–1918, reprinted 1969. ML410 G5 A11.

Four issues only; most of the contents are cited separately.

No. 1, 1913 (published 1914), 98 pp.

No. 2, 1915 (published 1916), 116 pp.

No. 3, 1917 (published 1917), 114 pp.

No. 4, 1918 (published 1918), 172 pp.

88. *Die Musik* 13/9 (1913–1914). 64 pp. plus 16 plates. ML5 M9.

Special Gluck issue; contents cited separately.

89. *La revue musicale: bulletin français de la Société Internationale de Musique* 10/6 (1914). 50 pp., including 15 plates. ML5 R613.

Special Gluck issue; contents cited separately.

IV

Biographical Studies and Dictionary Entries

90. Abert, Anna Amalie. "Von Wien nach Paris." *Gluck in Wien* (item 81), pp. 81–84.

    Brief but perceptive account of Gluck's move to Paris in the 1770s, examining the reasons for the move and comparing his reception in the two capitals.

91. ———. "Gluck." *Die Musik in Geschichte und Gegenwart*, ed. Fredrich Blume. Kassel: Bärenreiter, vol. 5 (1956), cols. 320–380. ML100 M92.

    Comprehensive dictionary entry, divided into biography, work list, stylistic analysis, list of editions, and bibliography. This perceptive analytical study demonstrates Gluck's individuality from the earliest operas, without making unrealistic claims for precocious reform tendencies. The fruitful influences of *opéra-comique* and ballet are persuasively argued.

92. ———. *Christoph Willibald Gluck*. Munich: Bong, 1959, reprinted Zurich: Buchergilde Gutenberg, 1960. 288 pp. ML410 G5 A55.

    Major biographical study. Many details of Gluck's relationships with his contemporaries established for the first time. Shows Gluck as continuously experimenting, each reform work operating a further, separate reform.

93. Anon. *Christoph Willibald Gluck: eine Biographie*. Kassel: Ernst Balde, 1855. 73 pp.

    Brief biography focusing on the reform works. Quotes extensively from contemporary documents, including several poems in praise of Gluck not readily available in more modern studies.

94. Antonicek, Theophil. "Glucks Existenz in Wien." *Gluck in Wien* (item 81), pp. 31–41.

Pieces together the sparse evidence on Gluck's life in Vienna, focusing on the patronage he enjoyed and the positions held.

95. Boer, Bertil van. "The Travel Diary of Joseph Martin Kraus: Translation and Commentary." *Journal of Musicology* 8/2 (1990): 266–290. ISSN 0277 9269. ML1 J693.

Records Kraus's visits to Gluck in 1783; informative on Gluck's reputation and his collaboration with Salieri on *Les Danaïdes*.

96. Brauneis, Walther. "Gluck in Wien—seine Gedenkstätten, Wohnungen und Aufführungsorte." *Gluck in Wien* (item 81), pp. 42–61.

Valuable study of dwellings occupied by Gluck in and around Vienna throughout his life, together with the theaters where he worked; well supported by contemporary engravings, ground plans, and maps.

97. Brook, Barry S. "Piraterie und Allheilmittel bei der Verbreitung von Musik im späten 18. Jahrhundert." *Beiträge zur Musikwissenschaft* 22 (1980): 217–239. ISSN 0005 8106. ML5 B352.

Examines the conditions in which piracy flourished and the part it played in the diffusion of scores. Notes the enormous financial rewards that publication and performance brought Gluck in Paris in the 1770s.

98. Brown, Bruce Alan. "Maria Theresa's Vienna." *The Classical Era: From the 1740s to the End of the 18th Century*, ed. Neal Zazlaw (*Man & Music*). London: Macmillan, 1989, pp. 99–125. ISBN 0 333 47260 8. ML195 C595 1989.

Relates genre and repertory to the institutions of theater, church, and concerts in Vienna in Gluck's lifetime.

99. Brown, Bruce Alan, and Julian Rushton. "Gluck, Christoph Willibald, Ritter von." *The New Grove Dictionary of Music and Musicians*, 2nd ed., ed. Stanley Sadie. London: Macmillan, 2001. ISBN 03336 08003. ML100 N48 2001.

Substantial dictionary entry comprising biographical sketch with essays on the different genres. The work list is the most up-to-date available, providing library sources for manuscript copies of unpublished works. Extensive bibliography. *New Grove* is available online at www.grovemusic.com.

100. Buchner, Franz Xaver. *Das Neueste über Christof Willibald Ritter von Gluck*. Kallmünz: Oberpfalz-Verlag 1915. 36 pp. ML410 G5 B83.

Establishes the errors and omissions in previous biographical studies, especially Schmid (item 144). Aims to correct the traditional account of Gluck's father's career, the houses occupied by the Gluck family, the baptismal record, and Gluck's immediate ancestors. A pioneer work in its time, expanded by Gerber (item 114). Includes family tree, pp. 33–36.

101. Buzga, Jaroslav. "Der junge Christoph Willibald Gluck bei den Prager Jesuiten." *Festschrift Klaus Hortschansky zum 60. Geburtstag*, ed. Axel Beer. Tutzing: Schneider, 1995, pp. 181–192. ISBN 3 7952 0822 X. ML55 H646 1995.

Investigates musical life in Prague in the years when Gluck was a student. Identifies the music Gluck could have heard, including oratorios, Jesuit plays, Italian operas, and music for the procession of ships on the Moldau.

102. Croll, Gerhard. "Der 'alte Gluck' und Mozart in Wien." *Gluck in Wien* (item 81), pp. 158–165.

Traces the events of Gluck's life in the 1780s, exploring the relationship between Gluck and Mozart; argues that Gluck's influence can be detected in *Die Entführung*.

103. ———. "Gluck in Wien, 1762: Zwischen *Don Juan* und *Orfeo ed Euridice*." *Traditionen-Neuansatze: für Anna Amalie Abert (1906–1996)*. Tutzing: Schneider, 1997, pp. 137–144. ML55 T75 1997.

Traces Gluck's activities and contacts in Vienna in 1762. Identifies a lost ballet, *La Citera assiedata*, performed on September 15, 1762, and includes Gasparini's program for it.

104. Ditters von Dittersdorf, Carl. *Lebensbeschreibung*. Leipzig, 1801, reprinted Munich: Kösel Verlag, 1967. 359 pp. ML410 D6 A3 1967. Trans. A. D. Coleridge as *The Autobiography of Karl von Dittersdorf*. London: Richard Bently, 1896, reprinted New York: Da Capo Press, 1970. 316 pp. ISBN 306 71864 2. ML410 D6 A33 1970.

An authentic eyewitness portrait of Gluck. Many details of contemporary musical life; valuable descriptions of the staging of *Le cinesi* (mistakenly referred to as *La danza*) at Schlosshof; informative on Gluck's visit to Italy in 1755–1756.

105. Dlabač, Jan Bohumir (Gottfried Johann Dlabcž). "Christoph Willibald Ritter von Gluck." *Allgemeine historisches Künstler-Lexikon für Böhmen*. Prague: Haase, 1815, vol. 1, cols. 469–476. N6837 D6.

An early dictionary entry, closely derived from Gerber (item 112) with some expansion of the biography. Quotes the preface to *Alceste*. Includes a work list and brief bibliography.

106. Edwards, F. R. G. "Gluck in England." *The Musical Times* 49 (1908): 508–513. ISSN 0027 4666. ML5 M85.

Soundly documented description of Gluck's visit to London in 1745. Quotes extensively from Burney (item 11) and from contemporary advertisements to establish performance data for *La caduta de'giganti* and *Artamene*. Notes the publication in London by Walsh of the six trio sonatas and excerpts from the two operas.

107. Einstein, Alfred. *Gluck*. Trans. Eric Blom. London: Dent, 1936. 2nd ed., 1964, reprinted New York: McGraw-Hill, 1972. ix, 238 pp. ISBN 0 070 19530 7. ML410 G5 E5 1972.

Perceptive biography in the useful format of the Master Musicians series, with a calendar of Gluck's life and an annotated biographical index, and substantial bibliography. Some stylistic analysis marred by outdated assumptions. In urgent need of revision.

108. ———. "Ein Schüler Glucks." *Acta musicologica* 10 (1938): 48–50. ISSN 0001 6241. ML5 I6.

A study of Karl Hanke, taught by Gluck in Vienna between 1772–1775. Quotes from the preface to Hanke's Singspiel, *Robert und Hannchen* (first performed in 1781 and printed in 1786 in Hamburg): a glowing tribute to Gluck's inspiration and tuition from a minor composer who stood to gain from associating himself with the successful Gluck.

109. Felix, Werner. *Christoph Willibald Gluck*. Leipzig: Reclam, 1965. 247 pp. ML410 G5 F4.

Wide-ranging biographical study, lavishly illustrated with contemporary theater designs, scores, autographs, etc. Based on Gerber (item 114) and Moser (item 190). Useful on the musical, social, and philosophical context of Gluck's stylistic development.

110. Funck, Heinrich. "Glucks zweimaliges Zusammentreffen mit Klopstock am Hofe Karl Friedrichs von Baden, 1774 und 1775." *Euphorion* 1 (1894): 790–792. PN4 D5.

Amplifies the account in Strauss (item 149) of Gluck's encounters with Klopstock in the mid-1770s, using the evidence of Riedel's letters.

111. Genlis, Stéphanie Félicité Ducrest de Saint Aubin. *Mémoires inédits de Madame la Comtesse de Genlis pour servir à l'histoire des dix-huitième et dix-neuvième siècles.* Paris: Colburn, 1825–1826. 8 vols. CT G287 G2.

Vols. 2–3 give an overview of life in Paris in the 1770s and offer evidence of partisan support for Gluck among society women. Two brief eyewitness accounts of Gluck at vol. 2, pp. 216–219 and vol. 3, p. 1.

112. Gerber, Ernst Ludwig. "Christoph von Gluck." *Historisch-biographisches Lexikon der Tonkünstler.* Leipzig: Breitkopf, 1790–1792, vol. 1, cols. 514– 518. 2nd ed., Leipzig: Kühnel, 1812–1814, reprinted Graz: Akademische Druck-und-Verlaganstalt, 1966. ML105 G38.

Dictionary entry containing one of the earliest assessments of Gluck's position in opera history. Discusses his rejection of Italian "*Schlendrian,*" and attributes his simplicity to the influence of his London visit and acquaintance with Arne. Quotes but dismisses criticism (Handel, Wolf) of Gluck's contrapuntal ability, drawing on Riedel (item 140) to support his argument. Identifies Gluck as a reformer of French music, driving the old French lyrical tragedy from the Parisian stage. Includes short list of published works.

113. Gerber, Rudolf. "Neue Beiträge zur Gluckschen Familiengeschichte." *Archiv für Musikforschung* 6 (1941): 129–150. ML5 A628.

New discoveries in Gluck family history research; research in this area was expanded by Schmitt (item 146).

114. ———. *Christoph Willibald Gluck.* Potsdam: Akademische Verlagsgesellschaft Athenaion, 1941. 2nd ed., 1950. 277 pp. Ml140 G5 G4.

Influential study, the basis of most subsequent biographies. Useful on Gluck's ancestry and early years (includes family tree). Perceptive analysis of Gluck's approach to characterization.

115. Grétry, André Ernest Modeste. *Mémoires; ou essais sur la musique.* Paris: Prault, 1789. 2nd ed., 1797, reprinted New York: Da Capo Press, 1971. 3 vols. ISBN 0 306 70194 4. ML410 G83 A3 1797a.

Offers a lively description of the mid-eighteenth-century musical scene. Perceptive comments on many contemporary musicians, including a warmly sympathetic view of Gluck.

116. Grossegger, Elisabeth. *Gluck und d'Afflisio. Ein Beitrag zur Geschichte der Verpachtung des Burgtheaters 1765/67–1776. Festgabe der Kommission für Theatergeschichte zum 75. Geburtstag Margret Dietrich.* Vienna:

Österreichische Akademie der Wissenschaften, 1995. 158 pp. ISBN 3 7001 2191 1. PN2616 V52 G59 1995.

Comments on the documents tracing Giuseppe d'Afflisio's period as impresario at the Burgtheater. Investigates Gluck's involvement with both the running of the theater and choice of program; documents his nearly ruinous involvement with d'Afflisio.

117. Heartz, Daniel. "Coming of Age in Bohemia: The Musical Apprenticeships of Benda and Gluck." *Journal of Musicology* 6/4 (1988): 510–527. ISSN 0277 9269. ML1 J693.

Investigates anecdotes of Gluck's childhood in the Bohemian countryside, his student years in Prague, and his move to Vienna in 1734 or 1735. See also Buzga (item 101), Howard (item 121), Mahler (item 131), and Mannlich (item 132).

118. ———. *Haydn, Mozart and the Viennese School.* New York, London: W. W. Norton, 1995. xxviii, 780 pp. ISBN 0 393 03712 6. ML246.8.V6H4.

Although a mere ninety pages directly address "Gluck and the Operatic Reform," this important volume offers a superbly detailed account of the social and cultural history of Gluck's Vienna. Particularly useful on the institutions of court and theatrical life.

119. ———. "Ditters, Gluck und der Artikel 'Von dem Wienerischen Geschmack in der Musik' (1766)." *Gluck in Wien* (item 81), pp. 78–80.

Takes further the discussion by Hass (in item 323), and plausibly attributes the article, with its lavish praise of Gluck, to Ditters.

120. Hortschansky, Klaus. "Gluck e la famiglia Absburgo Lorena." Trans. Giulio Cogni. *Chigiana* (item 86): 571–583.

Traces the development of Gluck's career in Vienna, particularly in relation to Hasse; establishes that Hasse was the more favored by Maria Theresa; investigates Gluck's relationship with other members of the imperial family, especially Archduke Leopold.

121. Howard, Patricia. "The Wandering Minstrel: An Eighteenth-Century Fiction." *Eighteenth-Century Fiction* 13/1 (2000): 41–52. ISSN 0840 6286. PN3495 E34.

Examines an episode in Gluck's youth narrated in Mannlich (item 132) and compares it with similar fictional narratives, concluding that Gluck's own account of a boyhood escapade was probably influenced by literary precedents, particularly George Primrose's travels in Oliver Goldsmith, *The Vicar of Wakefield.*

122. Karro, Françoise. "La rencontre du comte de Guibert et de Gluck." *Revue belge de musicologie* 44 (1990): 13–24. ISSN 0771 6788. ML5 R292.

    Records a meeting in Vienna, July 1773. Gluck, identified by Guibert as one of the greatest musicians in Europe, played scenes from *Iphigénie en Aulide* (compare Burney, item 10). Evidence of Gluck's ability to give a moving performance despite his rough singing voice, poor keyboard playing, and badly pronounced French. Notes Guibert's subsequent advocacy of Gluck's music.

123. Kinsky, Georg. "Glucks Reisen nach Paris." *Zeitschrift für Musikwissenschaft* 8 (1925–1926): 551–566. ML5 Z37.

    Establishes the timing and duration of Gluck's journeys to Paris between 1773 and 1779.

124. Kling, H. "Gluck als Dirigent." *Neue Zeitschrift für Musik* 86/40 (1890): 434–435. ML5 N4.

    Assembles brief eyewitness reports of Gluck as conductor and producer of his operas.

125. Kratochwill, Max. "Christoph Willibald Glucks Heiratskontrakt." *Jahrbuch des Vereins für Geschichte der Stadt Wien* 10 (1952–1953): 234–239. DB843 V38.

    An account of Gluck's marriage contract (text given) and associated documentary evidence from the Vienna Stadtsarchiv. Corrects previously held opinions concerning the relationship between Gluck and his future father-in-law and establishes a date for the latter's death.

126. Kretzschmar, Hermann. "Zum Verständnis Glucks." *Jahrbuch der Musikbibliothek Peters* 10 (1903): 61–76. ML5 J15.

    Biographical study supporting a perceptive appreciation of Gluck's dramatic genius and a plea for more performances of his work in the theater.

127. La Laurencie, Lionel de. "Gluck et sa réforme dramatique." *Encyclopédie de la musique et dictionnaire du Conservatoire.* Paris: Librairie Delagrave, 1913–1931, vol. 3, pp. 1425–1451. ML100 E5.

    Major dictionary entry. Biographical essay followed by a discussion of Gluck's style, focused almost extensively on the reform works. Analyzes the Paris operas in some detail, including interesting and original study of Gluck's use of rhythm in *Iphigénie en Aulide*.

128. Landormy, Paul. *Gluck*. Paris: Gallimard, 1941. 2nd ed., 1949. 246 pp. ML410 G5 L33.

   Biographical account biased toward the Paris period, based on sources in Tiersot (item 152).

129. Lipsius, Ida Maria (La Mara). *Christoph Willibald Gluck*. Leipzig: Breit-kopf & Härtel, 1868. 6th and 7th eds., 1923. 72 pp. ML410 G5 L4.

   Perceptive, trenchant biography, outstanding for its date. Rectifies many factual errors; work list revised and corrected in later editions.

130. Luca, Ignaz de. "Christoph Gluck." *Das gelehrte Oesterreich*. Vienna: Trattnern, 1777–1778, vol. 1, part 2, pp. 306–307.

   Short dictionary entry, interesting because of its early date. Evidence of Gluck's acknowledged position in Austria during the 1770s: "His *Alceste* and *Paride* alone would entitle him to the first place among the greatest musicians." Claims Gluck is working on settings of Klopstock's *Hermanns-Schlacht*, a *Stabat mater*, and Gellert's *Geistliche Lieder* (but see Rochlitz, item 142).

131. Mahler, Arnošt. "Glucks Schulzeit. Zweifel und Widersprüche in den bi-ographischen Daten." *Die Musikforschung* 27 (1974): 457–460. ISSN 0027 4801. ML5 M9437.

   Investigates problems and contradictions in earlier accounts of Gluck's years as a student.

132. Mannlich, Johann Christian von. *Histoire de ma vie*. Manuscript in D-Mbs Codex Gallicus 616–619, excerpted in "Mémoires sur la musique à Paris à la fin du règne de Louis XV." *La revue musicale* 16 (1934): 111–119, 161–171, 252–262. ML5 R613. A substantial extract, trans. Eugen Stoll-reither, as *Ein deutscher Maler und Hofmann: Lebenserinnerungen 1741–1822*. Mittler & Sohn, 1910. 568 pp.; shorter extract published in the origi-nal French as *Mémoires 1740–1822*. Paris: Calman Lévy, 1948. 308 pp. ND588 M17 A2.

   Indispensable biographical source. Contains intimate eyewitness accounts of Gluck, his appearance and personality, his composition methods, his collaboration with Moline, and vivid descriptions of the rehearsals of *Iphigénie en Aulide* and *Orphée*.

133. Marx, Adolf Bernhard. *Gluck und die Oper*. Berlin: Janke, 1863, reprinted Hildesheim: Olms, 1980. 794 pp. ML410 G5 M3.

     Comprehensive study based on Schmid (item 144), correcting some biographical data and ranging more widely in discussing the aesthetics of the reform and in analyzing the works. Includes eighty pages of music examples. Full bibliographical references in footnotes.

134. Mauclair, Camille, ed. "A travers la vie de Gluck." *La revue musicale* (item 89): 17–34.

     Symposium of brief contributions to Gluck biography: Löwenbach on Gluck's early years and the possibility of Bohemian influences in his music; Saint-Foix on the relationship between Gluck and Sammartini; Hammerich on Gluck's visit to Denmark in 1749; Vatielli on the performance of *Il trionfo di Clelia* in Bologna in 1763; Long on Gluck and Grétry.

135. Müller, Erich H. (Erich Hermann Mueller von Asow). "Gluck und die Brüder Mingotti." *Gluck-Jahrbuch* 3 (item 87): 1–14.

     Attempts to chronicle Gluck's career between 1746 and 1752 and to establish his involvement with the Mingotti troupe. See also Mueller von Asow (item 582).

136. Newman, Ernest. *Gluck and the Opera*. London: Dobell, 1895, reprinted New York: AMS Press, 1978. xxiv, 300 pp. ISBN 0 404 6 176 6. ML410 G5 N3 1978.

     The first full-length study of Gluck in English. Part I contains a biographical account, inevitably with many errors. Part II is an assessment of Gluck's achievements in relation to the cultural life of his age, Still worth reading for its analysis of the changing conventions of national opera (pp. 200–237) and contemporary aesthetic theories (pp. 238–296).

137. Prod'homme, Jacques-Gabriel. *Gluck*. Paris: Éditions SEFI, 1948. Revised and ed. by Joel-Marie Fauquet, Paris: Fayard, 1985. 413 pp. ISBN 221301 5759. ML410 G5 P65 1985.

     Major biographical study, thoroughly revised and updated by Fauquet. Particularly useful well-documented chapter on "La bataille parisienne," dealing with the period 1774 to 1779.

138. Prota-Giurleo, Ulisse. "Notizie biografiche intorno ad alcuni musicisti d'oltralpe a Napoli nel settecento." *Analecta musicologica* 2 (1965): 112–143. ISSN 0585 6086. ML160 S893.

Documentary study of music in Naples, referring to the following episodes in Gluck's life: the abortive proposal to perform *Arsace* and the substitution of *La clemenza di Tito*, the reception of *Tito*, and the performances of *Orfeo, Paride,* and *Alceste* in Naples in the 1770s. Also cites evidence that Gluck gave concerts on his glass harmonica in Naples in 1752.

139. Reichardt, Johann Friedrich. "Studien für Tonkünstler." *Musikalische Monatschrift* 3 (1792): 72–74. ML4 M45.

Constitutes Reichardt's additions to Gerber (item 112): a brief biographical sketch in the form of a series of anecdotes "from the hand of a Cavalier in Vienna." Chief interest lies in its early date and the possibility that some of the anecdotes either contain authentic eyewitness accounts of Gluck or originate from the composer himself.

140. Riedel, Fredrich Justus. *Ueber die Musik des Ritters Christoph von Gluck.* Vienna: Trattnern, 1775. xvi, 96 pp. ML410 G5 R42.

Contains a brief biography, identified by Wortsmann (item 48) as being the earliest biography of Gluck and the source on which Gerber (item 112) and Dlabač (item 105) are based. Four documents translated into German: letter from Arnaud to Madame d'Augny (see Lesure, item 336, vol. 1, pp. 29–39); letter to "Madame ***" on the subject of *Iphigénie en Aulide* (Lesure, vol. 2, pp. 9–27); conversation between Lully, Rameau, and Orpheus in the Elysian Fields (*Mercure de France* 1 (1774)); extract from the *Journal encyclopédique*, May 1774, on *Iphigénie*. Reviewed in Forkel (item 174).

141. Riegger, Joseph Stephan von, ed. "Gluck." *Materialen zur alten und neuen Statistik von Böhmen.* Leipzig, Prague: Widtmann, 1787–1793, vol. 12, p. 232.

Short dictionary entry, interesting as the first source to claim Gluck as a Bohemian composer. Inaccurate place of birth and date of death given.

142. [Rochlitz, Johann Friedrich.] "Glucks letzte Pläne und Arbeiten." *Allgemeine musikalische Zeitung* 25 (1809): cols. 385–390. ML5 A43.

Purports to interview an unnamed friend of Gluck's concerning doubtful or missing vocal works. Reports that there is no evidence that Gluck ever set *Stabat mater* or Gellert's *Geistliche Lieder* (see Luca, item 130). Argues that Gluck needed to find a text sympathetic in order to set it, and describes Gluck's close sympathy with Klopstock and Gluck's improvizations of Klopstock settings. Discusses the composition of *Hermanns-Schlacht*. See Salieri (item 143).

143. Salieri, Anton. "Erklärung in Beziehung auf Rochlitz's Aufsatz: Glucks letzte Pläne und Arbeiten." *Allgemeine musikalische Zeitung* 13 (1809): cols. 196–198. ML5 A43.

Responds to Rochlitz (item 142). Confirms that Gluck never set the *Stabat mater* and claims that *De profundis* was Gluck's only sacred work. Characterizes it as "not masterly (*maestralmente*) but Christian (*Cristianamente*)." Of Gluck's Klopstock settings, Salieri reports that only two short odes have been published. Suggests that *Hermanns-Schlacht* may never have been written down, on the grounds that he heard Gluck perform it several times but differently on each occasion.

144. Schmid, Anton. *Christoph Willibald Ritter von Gluck.* Leipzig: Fleischer, 1854. xii, 508 pp. ML410 G567.

A seminal work: the first full-length study of Gluck's life and works, soundly based and impressively documented. Includes information from Gluck's surviving relatives. Still useful as a source book. Appendices include documents, letters, and annotated bibliography.

145. Schmidt, Karl. "Eine musikalische Reise nach Wien 1772." *Die Musikerziehung* 33 (1980): 158–164. ML5 M9435.

Discusses Burney (item 10) describing the contents and orienting them for German-speaking readers. Deals in some detail with the encounter between Burney and Gluck.

146. Schmitt, Joseph. "Zur Familiengeschichte des berühmten Oberpfälzers Christoph W. Ritter von Gluck." *Verhandlung des historisches Vereins für Oberpfalz und Regensburg* 95 (1954): 215–225.

Summarizes the evidence for establishing Gluck's place of birth and accounts for the confusions surrounding these facts in early biographies. Investigates Gluck's ancestors. Schmitt's researches were developed by Gerber (item 114).

147. Seifert, Herbert. "Der junge Gluck—das musikdramatische Umfeld." *Gluck in Wien* (item 81), pp. 21–30.

While acknowledging our incomplete knowledge of the exact events of Gluck's youth, attempts to establish the repertory Gluck had the opportunity of encountering in Prague and Vienna up to his move to Milan in 1737. See also Buzga (item 101).

148. Stierlin, Leonhard. "Christoph Willibald Gluck." *Dreiundfünfzigstes Neujahrstück der allgemeinen Musikgesellschaft in Zürich.* Zurich: Orell, Füssli & Co., 1865. 28 pp. ML5 N48 No. 53.

Compact biographical study with some inaccuracies but useful for its insights into Gluck's relationships with Salieri and Reichardt.

149. Strauss, David Friedrich. "Klopstock und der Markgraf Karl Friedrich von Baden." *Kleine Schriften.* Leipzig: Brockhaus, 1862, pp. 23–67. 4PT Ger2644.

In the course of a biographical study of Klopstock's career and in particular his contact with Margrave Karl Friedrich von Baden, Strauss records an eyewitness account of Gluck's meeting with Klopstock in Karlsruhe in 1775. Includes a description of Gluck and his wife performing extracts from Klopstock's *Messias,* and of Marianne Gluck singing "Ich bin ein deutsches Mädchen." The meeting with Gluck (pp. 42–44) is reprinted in *Allgemeine musikalische Zeitung* 2/1 (1864): cols. 11–12. See Funck (item 110).

150. Tenschert, Roland. *Christoph Willibald Gluck. Der grosse Reformator der Oper.* Olten and Freiburg: Walter, 1951. 238 pp. ML410 G5 T28.

A compact biography followed by a useful collection of thirty-seven "Dokumente des Lebens" (pp. 169–215) which includes several contemporary accounts of Gluck by Reichardt, Dittersdorf, and Burney, the dedications to *Alceste, Paride ed Elena*, and *Orphée*, Gluck's birth, marriage, and death certificates, and many letters.

151. Tiersot, Julien. "Soixante ans dans la vie de Gluck (1714–1774)." *Le ménestrel* 73 (1907): 409, to 75 (1909): 98 *passim*. ML5 M465.

An extended study of Gluck's life up to 1774. Discusses current research and provides evidence of the state of Gluck studies at this period. Always illuminating on the music.

152. ———. *Gluck*. Paris: Alcan, 1910. 4th ed., 1919. 250 pp. Ml410 G5 T.

Biographical study with some analysis of the music. Biased towards the French operas, which Tiersot characterizes as Gluck's "œuvre definitive." Brief discussion of the desirability of a contralto in the role of Orpheus (pp. 136–140). For a French account of Gluck's work, Prod'homme (item 137) is preferable.

*Tocchini, Gerardo. *I fratelli d'Orfeo*. Cited as item 482.

153. Vauzanges, Louis M. "L'écriture de Gluck." *La revue musicale* (item 89): 35–38.

    Graphological analysis of Gluck's handwriting. Claims to trace his musical characteristics in his style of writing. See item 154.

154. ———. *Quelques musiciens vus à travers leur écriture.* Paris: Société de Graphologie, 1916. 23 pp.

    Graphological analysis: compares Gluck's handwriting with Piccinni's and claims to trace their opposing musical styles in their autographs.

V

General Studies in the Music

1. STUDIES IN GLUCK'S STYLE

155. Abert, Hermann, ed. "Das Musikdrama Glucks." *W. A. Mozart* (2nd ed. of Otto Jahn's biography, first published in 1856–1859). Leipzig: Breitkopf & Härtel, 1919–1921, vol. 1, pp. 675–696. ML410 M9 J5.

Deals with Gluck's stylistic development. Contrasts Gluck's cultivation of simplicity and his theories concerning the subordination of music to poetry with Mozart's attitudes to the same subjects. Disagreeing with Jahn's judgment in the 1st ed., contends that Gluck's characteristic style was not the result of his musical and technical limitations but the deliberate choice of a composer in the age of Enlightenment.

156. ———. "Wort un Ton in der Musik des 18. Jahrhunderts." *Archiv für Musikwissenschaft* 5 (1923): 31–70. ISSN 0003 9292. ML5 A63.

A wide-ranging discussion of the relationship between words and music in song and opera in the eighteenth century. Places Gluck at the turning point between old and new attitudes to word-setting, between an appropriate, typical expression of universal experiences and an individual response to unique situations.

157. ———. "Gluck. Mozart und der Rationalismus." *Gesammelte Schriften und Vorträge*, ed. Friedrich Blume. Halle: Niemeyer, 1929, reprinted Tutzing: Schneider, 1968, pp. 311–345. ML60 A18 1968.

Investigates the concept of rationalism on the stage and in particular its effect on characterization. Traces Gluck's differing approaches in the Vienna and Paris operas. Argues that Gluck perfectly fulfills rationalist theories. Compares Gluck with Mozart and contends that the latter's attitude to character belongs to a later generation and differs sharply from Gluck's. Concludes that Gluck belongs to the dramatic tradition of Lessing and Schiller while Mozart's aims are more akin to those of Herder and Goethe.

158. Arend, Max. "Glucks Orchester—vorklassisch?" *Musikalisches Wochenblatt* 35/40 (1904): 702–703. ML5 M92.

Brief but significant examination of Gluck's orchestration, which Arend defines as classical rather than preclassical, that is, the score represents the precise sound Gluck intended and is not to be augmented or filled in.

159. ———. *Gluck*. Berlin: Schuster & Loeffler, 1921. 278 pp. ML410 G5 A73.

Biographical content is now superseded. Worth reading for the perceptive discussion on the operas, though Arend tends to look with groundless zeal for signs of the reform in the early operas.

160. Baethge, Wilhelm. "Untersuchungen zum Erbe Erbeaneigung: Christoph Willibald Gluck." *Der Komponist und sein Adressat*, ed. Siegfried Bimberg. Halle: Martin Luther Universität, 1977, pp. 100–106. ML160 K828 1976.

A Marxist approach: argues that Gluck's creative ideals were oriented towards the bourgeois ideals of the Enlightenment. Identifies Gluck's importance for a present-day audience as consisting in his realistic depiction of individuals and in his breaking down of national styles and outdated conventions.

161. Baumann, Thomas. "Benda, the Germans, and Simple Recitative." *Journal of the American Musicological Society* 34 (1981): 119–131. ISSN 0003 0139. ML27 U5 A83363.

Analyzes attitudes in mid-eighteenth-century Germany to simple recitative as discussed by Georg Benda in an essay in Cramer's *Magazin der Musik* (item 16). Clarifies the usage of "simple" and "*secco*" among eighteenth-century writers and shows Gluck's rejection of the medium to be a reflection of widely held critical views.

162. Berlioz, Hector. *Grand traité d'instrumentation et d'orchestration modernes*. Paris: Lemoine, 1843. 2nd ed., Paris: Schonenberger, 1855. 321 pp. MT70 B48. Trans. Cowden Clarke as *A Treatise upon Modern Instrumentation and Orchestration*. London: Novello, 1856. MT70 B49 C7.

Numerous examples of Gluck's orchestration quoted and analyzed, with illuminating comments on nineteenth-century performances of Gluck's works, for example Habanek's *"tremolo près du chevalet"* in the Oracle scene in *Alceste* (pp. 7–18).

163. Bertrand, Jean-Edouard-Gustave. *Les nationalités dans le drame lyrique.* Paris: Didier, 1872. xxxi, 364 pp. ML1700 B37.

Examines the concept of national styles in opera from the Querelle des Bouffons to the later nineteenth century, pointing up the dichotomy between Gluck's reform theories and his Italianate practice. Analyzes *Alceste*, finding the libretto monotonous but praising the human expression in the vocal line. Discusses the criticisms of Rousseau (item 348), and Grétry (item 115).

164. Betzwieser, Thomas. "Musical Setting and Scenic Movement: Chorus and *chœur dansé* in Eighteenth-Century Parisian Opera." *Cambridge Opera Journal* 12/1 (2000): 1–28. ISSN 0954 5867. Expanded version of "Der in Bewegung gesetzte Chor: Gluck und der *chœur dansé.*" *D'un opéra l'autre: Hommage à Jean Mongrédien,* ed. Jean Gribenski, Marie-Claire Mussat, and Herbert Schneider. Paris: Presses Universitaires de France, 1996, pp. 45–54. ISBN 2 840 50063 9.

A major study. Argues that in Gluck's French operas, a new style of danced choruses constituted an important advance. Traces the evolution of the style from static, closed numbers in Lullian *tragédie lyrique* to dramatically functioning movements in Gluck's Paris operas. Attributes two innovations to Gluck: the integration of the chorus, which, under Gluck, used expressive gesture, with the corps de ballet, and the use of contrapuntal textures in *chœur dansé,* which had hitherto been associated with homophonic textures. Betzwieser's claim that Gluck first used "specific interplay" of chorus and dance in the Paris operas cannot be sustained (see Ricci, item 586).

165. Botstiber, Hugo. *Geschichte der Ouverture und der freien Orchesterformen.* Leipzig: Breitkopf & Härtel, 1913. 274 pp. ML1261 B68.

Traces the development of the overture from the Renaissance to the twentieth century. Cites theoretical discussions by Mattheson, Quantz, Scheibe (item 36), Algarotti (item 1), Planelli (item 33), and Rousseau (item 348). Identifies the unique place of *Alceste* in the history of the program overture and discusses the changes made to the *Telemaco* overture in adapting it for *Armide.* Argues, however, that Gluck's early overtures show no signs of his later achievements and are in fact more primitive than those of his contemporaries. Includes thirty-six pages of music examples.

166. Brown, Bruce Alan. *Gluck and the French Theatre in Vienna.* Oxford: Clarendon Press, 1991. xvii, 525 pp. ISBN 0 19 316415 9. ML1723.8.V6B76.

Major study of Gluck's involvement with the French theater in Vienna. Topics investigated include concerts, ballet, and *opéras-comiques*, setting *Don Juan* and *Orfeo* in the context of the repertory of the Burgtheater. Rich in primary sources presented in their original languages; informative about performers and the reception of Gluck's middle-period works. Based on item 489.

167. Bücken, Ernst. "Gluck." *Musik des Rokokos und der Klassik*. Potsdam: Akademische Verlagsgesellschaft Athenaion, 1928, pp. 174–191. ML160 B9.

Discusses Gluck's stylistic development and the relationship of his early works to the reform operas. Argues for the organic continuity of Gluck's whole output while acknowledging the distance between the youthful and the mature works. Sees Gluck as fulfilling the reform tendencies already present in Italian and French music and as discovering a new role for German dramatic music.

168. Capri, Antonio. "Che farò senza Euridice?" *La scala* 18 (1951): 28–32. ML5 S24.

Brief but widely ranging account of Gluck's reform. Attributes a major role to Calzabigi in releasing Gluck from conventional approaches. Assesses the influence of the *opéras-comiques* and the early *Lied* in forming Gluck's intimate style. Discusses Gluck in relation to Monteverdi and Wagner, asserting that Gluck has more affinity with the earlier composer through his "*aura d'ellenismo*" and his universality of expression.

169. Cooper, Martin. *Gluck*. London: Chatto & Windus, 1935. xv, 293 pp. ML410 G5 C5.

Biographical material now superseded but contains perceptive analysis of Gluck's changing musical style. Generously illustrated with music examples both from Gluck's scores and from those of his contemporaries.

170. Corte, Andrea della. *Gluck e suoi tempi*. Florence: Sansoni, 1948. 213 pp. ML410 G5 C54.

Examines Gluck's ambivalent position in operatic history, pointing up the variety of artistic attitudes he held and relating these to the environment of reform. Explores Calzabigi's influence on Gluck's concept of declamation and dramatic structure. Slight coverage of the earlier operas but gives detailed consideration to the reform works. The many illustrations from twentieth-century Italian productions make this a useful source for recent stage history.

171. Downes, Edward O. D. "Secco Recitative in Early Classical Opera Seria, 1720–80." *Journal of the American Musicological Society* 14 (1961): 50–69. ISSN 0003 0139. ML27 U5 A83363.

Discusses widely differing contemporary evaluations of the musical and dramatic effect of *secco* recitative. Argues, with many music examples, that Gluck's finest *secco* writing dates from around 1750.

172. Finscher, Ludwig. "'Che farò senza Euridice?' Ein Beitrag zur Gluck-Interpretation." *Festschrift Hans Engel zum 70. Geburtstag*, ed. Horst Heussner. Kassel: Bärenreiter, 1964, pp. 96–110. ML55 E52 H5.

Deals with the conflicting reactions to "Che farò" expressed both by Gluck's contemporaries and later critics. Examines the sources and variants of the aria, especially tempo, dynamic, and articulation directions, in particular Guadagni's interpretation recorded by Corri (item 303). Argues that its expressive subtlety is the equal of Orestes's arioso "Le calme rentrer dans mon cœur."

173. ———. "Gluck e la tradizione dell'opera seria. Il problema del lieto fine nei drammi della riforma." Trans. Giulio Cogni. *Chigiana* (item 86): 263–274.

Discusses the convention of *lieto fine*, distinguishing three aspects: aversion in eighteenth-century theater to portraying death on the stage, the requirement of a mythological plot to be resolved "from above," and the special role of *lieto fine* in opera seria as conflict resolved through an unforeseen turn of events. Analyzes the conclusions of *Orfeo*, *Alceste*, and *Iphigénie en Aulide* as three uniquely individual dramatic solutions to the need for a resolution in tragedy.

174. Forkel. Johann Nicolaus. "Ueber die Musik des Ritters Christoph von Gluck." *Musikalische-kritische-Bibliothek*. Gotha: C. W. Ettinger, 1778, vol. 1, pp. 53–173. ML4 M31.

Review of Riedel (item 140). Trenchantly attacks Gluck's reputation and uncritical adulation of his works; contests the role ascribed to him by Riedel as instigator of the reform and argues that Gluck's aims are in conflict with the very nature of music. Compare Schubart (item 354).

175. Garlington, Aubrey Sam. "'Le merveilleux' and Operatic Reform in Eighteenth-century French Opera." *The Musical Quarterly* 49 (1963): 484–497. ISSN 0027 4631. ML1 M725.

Discusses criticisms of the tradition of *"merveilleux"* by the Encyclope-dists. Analyzes examples of the supernatural in Gluck's reform operas, ar-guing that Gluck's musical style in scenes such as the infernal spirits in *Alceste* or the magic garden in *Armide* supports and is analogous with the visual effect. Traces the influence of Gluck's approach in works by Sac-chini, Salieri, Lemoyne, and Cherubini.

176. Geiringer, Karl. "Concepts of the Enlightenment as Reflected in Gluck's Italian Reform Operas." *Studies on Voltaire and the Eighteenth Century* 88 (1972): 567–576. PQ2105 A2 S8.

Overview of Gluck's dramatic style: discusses the theories Algarotti (item 1) and how they are taken up in Gluck's reform operas.

177. Goldschmidt, Hugo. "Zur Psychologie des Gluckschen Kunstschaffens." *Gluck-Jahrbuch* 3 (item 87): 15–24.

Examines Gluck's concept of opera and the matching of musical to verbal expression. Argues that Gluck did not in fact limit the role of music, de-spite claims in the *Alceste* preface. Some discussion of Rolland (item 256).

178. Hortschansky, Klaus. "Doppelvertonungen in den italienischen Opern Glucks. Ein Beitrag zu Glucks Schaffensprozess." *Archiv für Musikwis-senschaft* 24 (1967): 54–63, 133–144. ISSN 0003 9292. ML5 A63.

Deals with ten instances in Gluck's works where the composer reset an Italian aria text when revising the work for a revival. Divides the resettings into those made at the request of a performer and those where Gluck's mo-tive was apparently uninfluenced by external demands.

179. ———. *Parodie und Entlehnung im Schaffen Christoph Willibald Glucks.* Cologne: Volk, 1973. Vol. 13 of *Analecta musicologica.* viii, 340 pp. ISBN 3 87252 058 X. ML410 G5 H66.

Major study of Gluck's creative process, analyzing his parody technique and self-borrowings, all of which are tabulated and discussed. Indispens-able reading for a study of Gluck at any level.

180. Howard, Patricia. *Gluck and the Birth of Modern Opera.* London: Barrie & Rockliff, 1963. 118 pp. ML410 G5 H67.

Analyzes Gluck's contribution to the various components of opera—aria, recitative, chorus, ensemble, overture—and sets his achievements in the context of the wider reforms of opera and ballet in the mid-eighteenth cen-tury. Detailed study of Gluck's dramatic approach in *Iphigénie en Tauride.*

181. Istel, Edgar. "Gluck's Dramaturgy." Trans. Theodore Baker, *The Musical Quarterly* 27 (1931): 227–233. ISSN 0027 4631. ML1 M725.

   Assesses Gluck's position in the history of opera as a pivot between Monteverdi and Wagner. Discusses Gluck's aesthetic attitudes, referring to statements attributed to him by Corancez (item 302).

182. Kaufmann, Harald. "Orpheus zwischen Form und Ausdruck." *Österreichische Musikzeitschrift* 19/9 (1964): 409–421. ISSN 0029 9316. ML5 01983.

   Investigates the tension between form and expression in Gluck's reform operas, focused on the supernatural scenes in *Orfeo*, *Alceste*, and *Iphigénie en Tauride* and dealing principally with tonality, rhythm, and motif.

183. ———. "Gluck's Rückkehr zur Sprache." *Forum* 11 (1964): 619–621.

   Examines the general nature of declamation in the reform operas, with a specific study of examples from *Iphigénie en Aulide*; investigates Gluck's flexible handling of meter to reveal Agamemnon's changing psychological state. Identifies the *lieto fine* as a problem for modern producers to tackle.

184. Klinger, Kurt. "Gluck e l'illuminismo austriaco." Trans. Giulio Cogni. *Chigiana* (item 86): 247–261. Revised as "Gluck und der aufgeklärte Absolutismus in Österreich," in *Christoph Willibald Gluck und die Opernreform* (item 83), pp. 353–372.

   Relates Gluck's reforms to the cultural context of the Austrian Enlightenment and the coincidence of political, social, and artistic aims: "reforms are the theme of the century." Examines the dramatic structures of Gluck's reform operas and argues that their chief significance is in bringing opera seria to its highest point of development.

185. Koller, Walter. "Zur Rolle der Instrumente in der textgebundenen Musik Christoph Willibald Glucks." *Aus der Werkstatt der Wiener Klassiker*, ed. Helmut Hell. Tutzing: Schneider, 1975, pp. 181–220. ISBN 3 7952 0158 6. ML455 K64.

   Bases his survey on examples of Gluck's orchestration selected by Berlioz in his *Grand traité* (item 162). Compares Gluck's and Bertoni's settings of *Orfeo*, Gluck's and Lully's settings of *Armide*, and Gluck's setting of "Io non chiedo" (*Alceste*) with Mozart's setting of the same text in Scena, K 316. Notes Gluck's use of tremolo and vibrato, with reference to Schenk (item 201), relating the techniques to word-setting.

186. Landon, H. C. Robbins. "Some Thoughts on Gluck and the Reform of the Opera." *Essays on the Viennese Classical Style: Gluck, Haydn, Mozart, Beethoven.* London: Barrie & Rockliff, 1970, pp. 22–38. ISBN 214 667944. ML60 L225 E9.

Argues that the traditional concept of Gluck's reform is a myth, that Gluck did not reform more than a small area of the whole field of opera, and that he failed to have any impact on the "really important operatic form of the second part of the eighteenth century," that is, opera buffa. Suggests that Mozart could be considered far more influential in opera reform.

187. Lavoix, Henri. *Histoire de l'instrumentation depuis le seizième siècle jusqu'à nos jours.* Paris: Didot, 1878, pp. 311–328. ML455 L41.

Brief but interesting survey of Gluck's orchestration both in terms of the instruments employed and the effect on the audience.

188. Meyer, Ralph. "Die Behandlung des Rezitativs in Glucks italienischen Reformopern." *Gluck-Jahrbuch* 4 (item 87): 1–90.

Major study of the development of eighteenth-century recitative. Argues that the increased expressive content of *secco* and the introduction of declamation into the aria in the Italian Reform operas led eventually to the homogeneous style of the Paris operas. An overview of recitative in the pre-*Orfeo* operas is followed by detailed studies of recitative in *Orfeo, Alceste,* and *Paride ed Elena.*

189. Mioli, Piero. "Sulle ali del canto nell'aria: osservazioni sulla forma dell'aria e sulla scrittura del canto." *Christoph Willibald Gluck nel 200° anniversario della morte* (item 82), pp. 497–509.

Argues that *bel canto* style, closed aria forms, and the association of certain voice types with roles are all characteristic of Italian opera throughout the mid-seventeenth to mid-nineteenth centuries; examines how far Gluck worked to reform the tradition, noting new aria forms and voice roles from *Alceste* onwards.

190. Moser, Hans Joachim. *Christoph Willibald Gluck. Die Leistung, der Mann, das Vermächtnis.* Stuttgart: Cotta, 1940. xv, 369 pp. ML410 G5 M6.

Investigates Gluck's developing style in the context of contemporary theater conventions. Particularly valuable for its melodic and tonal analysis of the works before *Orfeo.*

191. Müller-Blattau, Josef. "Gluck und die deutsche Dichtung." *Jahrbuch der Musikbibliothek Peters* 45 (1938): 30–52. ML5 J15.

Describes the impact of Klopstock's renewal of German poetry on German musicians and argues that Gluck encountered the Odes at just the right time in his career (between his Vienna and Paris reform operas) to respond to their style. Documents Gluck's relationship with Klopstock. Compares Gluck's settings of French and German texts in connection with his and Alxinger's translation of *Iphigénie en Tauride*, arguing that Gluck's handling of the translation reveals him to be a poet of some talent.

192. Neumann, Frederick. "The Appoggiatura in Mozart's Recitative." *Journal of the American Musicological Society* 35 (1982): 115–137. ISSN 0003 0139. ML27 U5 A83363.

Discusses Gluck's ornamentation in *Orfeo* and notes where it differs from that advocated by Corri (item 303). Relates theoretical writings (e.g., by Tosi, item 37, and Mancini, item 25) to the evidence of the scores.

193. Owen, Angela Maria. "The Chalumeau and its Music." *American Recorder* 8/1 (1967): 7–9. ML27 U5 A8343.

Examines the use of the chalumeau in eighteenth-century operas and cantatas. Notes Gluck's exploitation of its special tone qualities in *Orfeo*.

194. Pannuti, Ulrico. "La 'riforma' di Gluck." *La scala* 91 (June 1957): 26–29. ML5 S24.

Argues that Gluck's most striking reform was his approach to orchestration, as acknowledged by Berlioz (item 162). Cites examples from the reform operas and *De profundis* to illustrate Gluck's originality as an orchestrator.

195. Parkinson, John. "The Barbaric Unison." *The Musical Times* 114 (1973): 23–24. ISSN 0027 4666. ML5 M85.

Discusses the use of unison textures in *Orfeo* and in works by Vivaldi, Bach, Handel, and Beethoven. Argues that in baroque and classical style conventions, harmony represents order, civilization, and a sense of divine purpose, whereas unison is often used to represent the barbaric.

196. Pierce, Terry. "The Trombome in the Eighteenth Century." *Journal of the International Trombone Association* 8 (1980): 6–10. ISSN 0145 3513. ML1 I86.

In a technical survey of the development of the trombone, briefly examines Gluck's pioneering role in bringing trombones back into the opera orchestra and his dramatic exploitation of their tone color.

197. Robinson, Michael. "The Aria in opera seria 1725–1780." *Proceedings of the Royal Musical Association* 88 (1961–1962): 31–43. ML28 L8 M8.

Traces changing attitudes to form and style in eighteenth-century arias. Shows how Gluck's rejection of the da capo and advocacy of simplicity paralleled developments in unreformed opera seria.

198. Rosen, Charles. *The Classical Style.* London: Faber & Faber, 1971. 2nd ed., 1976. 467 pp. ISBN 0 571 04905 2. ML195 R68 1976.

Detailed study of late-eighteenth-century style, focused on Haydn, Mozart, and Beethoven but containing (pp. 169–180) a perceptive analysis of Gluck as a neoclassical composer.

199. Rossini, Paolo. "Gli strumenti della drammaturgia gluckiana: orchestra, coro, danza." *Christoph Willibald Gluck nel 200° anniversario della morte* (item 82), pp. 475–496.

Argues that Gluck can be regarded as the founder of modern orchestration. Selects as landmarks in Gluck's development the fuller orchestral writing in *La clemenza di Tito*, the innovative use of brass in *Don Juan*, and the search for new timbres in the reform operas. Notes the variety of roles for the chorus in *Orfeo*, and the ballet in *Alceste*.

200. Rushton, Julian. "Christoph Willibald Gluck, 1714–87: The Musician Gluck." *The Musical Times* 128 (1987): 615–618. ISSN 0027 4666. ML5 M85.

Argues that Gluck's purely musical abilities have often been overshadowed by his power as dramatist; defends Gluck as "a representative musician of the Age of Enlightenment" by illustrating the breadth of styles he mastered and the refinement of detail in their execution.

201. Schenk, Erich. "Zur Aufführungspraxis des Tremolo bei Gluck." *Anthony van Hoboken: Festschrift zum 75. Geburtstag*, ed. Joseph Schmidt-Görg. Mainz: B. Schotts Söhne, 1962, pp. 137–145. ML55 H6 S3.

Examines the evidence concerning the performance of tremolo in the eighteenth century. Discusses the variety of notation used and the confusion between tremolo, *ondeggiando*, and vibrato. Argues that the three devices were clearly differentiated in terms of *Affekt* and usage.

202. Schneider, Herbert. "Gluck als 'prosateur en musique.'" *Festschrift Klaus Hortschansky zum 60. Geburtstag*, ed. Axel Beer. Tutzing: Schneider, 1995, pp. 193–209. ISBN 3 7952 0822 X. ML55 H646 1995.

Traces the fashion in France for the asymmetric as aesthetic goal. Argues that symmetry was seen in arts as diverse as ballet and landscaping to be unnatural and a barrier to the viewer's involvement; relates this to the informality and spontaneity of Gluck's French operas.

203. Schneider, Max. "Die Begleitung des Secco-Rezitativs um 1750." *Gluck-Jahrbuch* 3 (item 87): 88–107.

Investigates how recitative was accompanied in the midcentury, using the evidence of numerous contemporary accounts. Argues for simplicity and harmonic clarity and suggests taking the plainer passages of accompanied recitative as models.

204. Staiger, Emil. "Glucks Bühnenkunst." *Christoph Willibald Gluck und die Opernreform* (item 83), pp. 39–49.

Attempts to relate the portrayal of the "antique" in Gluck's reform operas to both Greco-roman and eighteenth-century dramatic practice.

205. Sternfeld, Frederick W. "Gluck's Operas and Italian Tradition." *Chigiana* (item 86): 275–281.

Argues the continuity of musical and dramatic tradition from sixteenth-century *intermedi* to Gluck's Viennese masterpieces; examines the debt Gluck's finales owe to the Italian *festa teatrale*. See also Monelle (item 248), Leopold (item 397), and Joly (item 551).

206. Tiersot, Julien. "Gluck and the Encyclopædists." Trans. Theodore Baker. *The Musical Quarterly* 16 (1930): 336–357. ISSN 0027 4631. ML1 M725.

Discusses the intellectual background to the reform in Vienna and Paris. Contends that in his Paris operas Gluck responded to a sympathetic climate of thought created by the writers of the *Encyclopédie* and fulfilled their aesthetic aspirations, voiced several decades earlier.

207. Tovey, Donald Francis. "Christoph Willibald Gluck (1714–87) and the Musical Revolution of the Eighteenth Century." *The Heritage of Music*. Oxford and London: Oxford University Press, 1934, vol. 2, pp. 69–117, reprinted in *Essays and Lectures on Music*. Oxford and London: Oxford University Press, 1949, pp. 65–102. ML60 T665 1949.

An assessment of Gluck's status as a composer. Although some factual statements are now known to be erroneous and some artistic judgments are inevitably dated, this account remains worth reading for its penetrating examination of the reform operas.

208. Udine, Jean d' (Albert Cozanet). *Gluck.* (*Les musiciens célèbres.*) Paris: Renouard, 1906. 2nd ed., 1930. 124 pp. ML410 G5 C6.

Aims to place Gluck in the context of his contemporaries but analyzes his style from the point of view of the early twentieth century. Includes interesting illustrations of eighteenth- and nineteenth-century stage designs.

209. ———. "Les arts synesthésiques—la musique pittoresque et sentimentale." *L'art et le geste,* pp. 69–86. Paris: Alcan, 1910.

Investigates the relationship between music and gesture. Defines three sorts of melody (recitative, declamatory, and lyrical) and shows, in a brief analysis of Act II of *Armide,* how Gluck's melodic style suggests appropriate gestures by the singers.

210. Vatielli, Francesco. "Riflessi della lotta Gluckista in Italia." *Rivista musicale italiana* 21 (1914): 639–674. Ml5 R66.

Traces Gluck's reputation in Italy through letters addressed to Padre Martini. Examines how far Gluck's reform operas can still be called "Italian operas"; concludes that his more "rugged" passages belong to a new, Germanic, operatic style.

211. Vetter, Walther. "Christoph Willibald Gluck." *Mythos-Melos-Musica* (item 84), vol. 1, pp. 293–297.

Notes the significance of the London trio sonatas in Gluck's development and the achievement of the Klopstock settings. Discusses the extent of his influence on nineteenth-century composers.

212. ———. "Zur Stilproblem der italienischen Oper des 17. und 18. Jahrhunderts." *Studien zur Musikwissenschaft* 15 (1962): 561–573. Ml55 S9.

Follows Wölfflin (see also items 213 and 270) in seeing an irreconcilable difference between North and South (German and Italian) attitudes to art. Argues that Italian opera serves ideals of nature, feeling, and impulse; German opera, while acknowledging the force of these, is also concerned with spirit, reason, and understanding. Compares Gluck's reform operas with those of Metastasio and argues that the significance Gluck's achievement lay in his building of large-scale structures rather than in the replacement of the da capo aria with smaller aria types.

213. ———. *Christoph Willibald Gluck: ein Essay.* Leipzig: Deutscher Verlag für Musik, 1964. 198 pp. ML410 G5 V5.

Stimulating and individual account. Takes as its starting point Hoffmann's romantic fantasy (item 326). Relates Gluck to German classicism, contrasting his development with that of Goethe and Schiller. Discusses Gluck's musical roots in the music of his Bohemian, Italian, and German contemporaries. Adapts Wölfflin's thesis of style relationships in art history to examine Gluck's assimilation of different styles. Includes a perceptive chapter on *Écho et Narcisse*.

214. Wellesz, Egon. "Three Lectures on Opera: The Problem of Form." *Essays on Opera*, trans. Patricia Kean. London: Dobson, 1950, pp. 90–106. ML1700 1 W42.

    Explores the problem of form in opera, investigating Gluck's solution of opera as a "unified vision of continuously relevant music, architecturally structured."

215. Westrup, Jack Allen. "The Nature of Recitative." *Proceedings of the British Academy* 52 (1956): 27–43. ISSN 0068 1202. AS122 L5.

    Wide-ranging account touching on the forms and functions of recitative from Caccini to Britten. Identifies a crisis in eighteenth-century recitative and argues that Gluck was crucial in resolving it.

216. Würtz, Roland. "Das Türkische im Singspiel des 18. Jahrhunderts bis zu Mozarts *Entführung aus dem Serail*." *Wiener Figaro* 47 (June 1980): 8–14.

    Develops Preibisch's study (item 496). Traces the history of the Turkish convention in the eighteenth century, focusing on the characteristic instruments employed. Discusses Gluck's Turkish orchestration in *Le cadi dupé*, *La recontre imprévue*, and *Iphigénie en Tauride*.

2. GLUCK IN COMPARATIVE STUDIES

217. Abert, Hermann. *Niccolò Jommelli als Opernkomponist*. Halle: Max Niemeyer, 1908. 461, 64 pp. ML410 J7 A23.

    Detailed comparison between Jommelli and Gluck. Points up the greater simplicity and dramatic intensity of Gluck's approach and the richer and more elaborate style of Jommelli's work. Concludes that Jommelli had the musical perceptions but not the personality to be a reformer. Includes sixty-four pages of music examples.

218. ———. "Mozart and Gluck." Trans. C. B. Oldman. *Music & Letters* 10 (1929): 256–265. ISSN 0027 4224. ML5 M64.

    Argues that the dramatic aims of the two composers were divergent and that echoes of Gluck's music in Mozart are eclectic reminiscences rather than evidence of systematic and committed imitation. Contends that

Mozart most nearly approached the spirit of Gluck's reform in *Die Zauber-flöte*. See Croll (item 228).

219. Arend, Max. "Mozart in seinem Verhältnis zu Gluck." *Zur Kunst Glucks* (item 80), pp. 203–219.

Discusses the extent of Gluck's influence on Mozart from both a musical and a dramatic point of view. Analyzes the bias in Jahn's and Marx's arguments (items 155 and 133) and concludes that it is unrealistic to attempt to show an affinity between two geniuses whose uniqueness makes them incommensurable.

220. Baselt, Bernd. "Zum Thema Händel und Gluck." *Gluck in Wien* (item 81), pp. 139–150.

Traces the relationship between Handel and Gluck, arguing that Handel's oratorios prefigure many of the "reform" qualities of Gluck's mature operas, and seeks to prove that Gluck consciously sought to emulate Handel's melodic and harmonic style. See also Rackwitz (item 252).

221. Bimberg, Guido. "Dramaturgische Strukturmomente in den Ezio-Opern von Händel und Gluck." *Wissenschaftliche Konferenz zu den 26. Handelfestspielen der DDR*, ed. Walther Siegmund-Schulze. Halle: Wissenschaftliche Beiträge, Martin Luther Universität, 1977, pp. 41–46. AS182 H125 1976, 22.

Analyzes two settings of Metastasio's libretto. Argues that Handel sought to bring out contrasting emotions whereas Gluck explored the transition from one mood to another, but that in terms of dramatic structure Gluck's opera is highly conventional while Handel's attempts to transcend established patterns and formulas.

222. Bitter, Carl Hermann. *Die Reform der Oper durch Gluck und R. Wagners Kunstwerk der Zukunft*. Braunschweig: Vieweg, 1884. 339 pp. ML1704 B62.

Attempts to establish Gluck's reforms in the context of his contemporaries. Perceptive discussion of Gluck's debt to Handel, Lully, Rameau, Graun, Hasse, and Traetta; traces Wagner's debt to Gluck.

223. Blom, Eric, "A Misjudged Composer." *Stepchildren of Music*. London: Foulis, 1925, pp. 57–66. ML60 B67.

Compares Gluck and Piccinni. Contends that Piccinni's operas are inferior to Gluck's but nevertheless deserve recognition, and that Piccinni was Gluck's superior in fluency, craftsmanship, and harmonic skill. See Rushton (items 259 and 260).

224. Buelow, George J. "A Bach Borrowing by Gluck: Another Frontier." *Eighteenth-Century Music in Theory and Practice: Essays in Honor of Alfred Mann Stuyvesant*, ed. Mary Ann Parker. New York: Pendragon, 1994, pp. 187–203. ISBN 0 945 193114. ML55. M25 1994.

Discusses Gluck's use of the opening of the Gigue from Bach's Partita No. 1 in the aria appearing variously as "Perché se tanti siete" (*Antigono*), "Se a estinguer non bastate" (*Telemaco*), and "Je t'implore et je tremble" (*Iphigénie en Tauride*).

225. Bunghardt, Volker, "Josef Martin Kraus (1756–92). Ein Meister des klassischen Klavierliedes." Doctoral dissertation, University of Cologne, 1973. 271 pp.

Compares Kraus's songs with those of Haydn, Mozart, and Gluck: a detailed analytical study.

226. Buschmeier, Gabriele. *Die Entwicklung von Arie und Szene in der französischen Oper von Gluck bis Spontini.* Tutzing: Schneider, 1991. xi, 334 pp. ISBN 3 7952 0674 X. ML1727 B87 1991.

Major study of the dramatic and musical structures of French opera. Contrasts the Italian tradition of number opera with the long-standing tendency towards continuity in French opera, and traces the effect of this on the form and function of the aria. Places Gluck's development in the context of the French tradition and traces parallels in the music of Le Moyne, Piccinni, and Sacchini.

227. Churgin, Bathia. "Alterations in Gluck's Borrowings from Sammartini." *Studies in Music* 9/1 (1980): 117–134. ISSN 0081 8267. ML5 S9255.

Deals with instances of Gluck's borrowings from Sammartini. Contends that Gluck's attempts to alter the originals are unsuccessful. Detailed examination of the first movement of the overture to *Le nozze* and the introduction to Part II of *La contesa de'numi*.

228. Croll, Gerhard. "Gluck und Mozart." *Österreichische Musikzeitschrift* 28/7–8 (1973): 300–307. ISSN 0029 9316. ML5 01983.

Compares the two composers' personalities, artistic aims, and approaches to the composition process. Establishes many points of similarity between them and argues that it is in *Die Zauberflöte* that Mozart most nearly approaches Gluck. See Abert (item 218).

229. Degrada, Francesco. "Aspetti Gluckiani nell'ultimo Hasse." *Chigiana* (item 86): 309–329. Also in *Il palazzo incantato. Studi sulla tradizione del*

melodrama dal barocco al romanticismo. Fiesole: Discanto, 1972, vol. 1, pp. 132–154. ML1700 D43.

Discusses Hasse's setting of Coltellini's *Piramo e Tisbe*; argues that a different route to reform is evident in this libretto, influenced by the same climate of thought that molded Gluck but differing from his reforms in the perception of the role of the voice as the central vehicle for dramatic expression.

230. ———. "Due volti di Ifigenia." *Il palazzo incantato. Studi sulla tradizione del melodrama dal barocco al romanticismo*. Fiesole: Discanto, 1972, vol. 1, pp. 155–208. ML1700 D43.

Compares Gluck's and Piccinni's settings of *Iphigénie en Tauride*; includes appendix of documents on the Gluck-Piccinni controversy. See Rushton (item 260).

231. Dent, Edward J. "Italian Opera in the Eighteenth Century and its Influence on the Music of the Classical Period." *Sammelbände der Internationalen Musikgesellschaft* 14 (1912–1913): 500–509. ML5 I66.

Argues for a reassessment of opera seria and the dramatic ideals of Metastasio which Gluck studies tend to undervalue. Notes the achievements of Alessandro Scarlatti, Hasse, and Jommelli, in particular their development of the aria form.

232. Desnoiresterres, Gustave. *Gluck et Piccinni: la musique française au XVIIIᵉ siècle, 1774–1800*. Paris: Didier, 1872. 2nd ed., 1875. xi, 425 pp. ML1727 3 D41 1875.

Well-documented account of the Gluck-Piccinni controversies. Valuable for the many quotations from the contemporary press with full bibliographical references. Argues that the rivalry between the two composers was fruitful for Piccinni, stimulating him to abandon his graceful style for a more dramatic one, this change being particularly evident in *Didon*.

233. Engländer, Richard. "Zu den Müchener Orfeo-Aufführungen 1773 und 1775." *Gluck-Jahrbuch* 2 (item 87): 26–55.

Discusses the sources relating to the versions of *Orfeo* given in Munich in 1773 and 1775. Closely compares the operas. Many music examples. See Cattelan (item 565).

234. ———. "Gluck-Pflege und Nachfolge Glucks in Schweden Gustavs III." *Musa-Mens-Musici im Gedenken an Walther Vetter*, ed. Heinz Wegener. Berlin: Institut für Musikwissenschaft der Humboldt-Universität, 1969, pp. 215–223.

Argues that Gluck's reforms influenced the Swedish poets in the reign of Gustav III. Examines the collaboration of the composer Josef Martin Kraus with the poet Klopstock and relates the reforms to the *Sturm und Drang* movement in literature. Compare Bunghardt (item 225).

235. Floros, Constantin. "Das 'Programm' in Mozarts Meister-ouvertüren." *Studien zur Musikwissenschaft* 26 (1964): 140–186. ML55 S9.

Traces the influence of Gluck on Mozart from *Idomeneo* onwards. Analyzes overtures to *Alceste* and *Iphigénie en Aulide*, both in their intrinsic structures and their thematic links with the operas. Investigates similar thematic links in Mozart. Argues that Mozart learned from Gluck to write overtures that form both a thematic and a psychological preparation for the operas they introduce.

236. Gallarati, Paolo. *Gluck e Mozart*. Turin: Einaudi, 1975. 151 pp. ML390 G149.

Contrasts Gluck the rationalist with Mozart the psychological realist. Traces, nevertheless, some stylistic relationships, above all in their treatment of the supernatural. Argues that Gluckian reminiscences exist in certain scenes in *Idomeneo, Don Giovanni*, and *Die Zauberflöte*.

237. Garda, Michela. "Da *Alceste* a *Idomeneo*: Le scene 'terribili.'" *Il saggiatore musicale* 1/2 (1994): 335–360. ISSN 1123 8615. ML5 S137.

Investigates the "terror" scenes in *Alceste, Iphigénie en Aulide*, and *Iphigénie en Tauride*, comparing them with similar scenes in *Idomeneo* and Jommelli's *Fetonte*. Argues that the concepts of the "terrible" and the "pathétique," mentioned in the letters of Gluck and Du Roullet, are subsumed in definitions of the "sublime" by Diderot, Schiller, and Kant, and that this aesthetic concept shaped the reception of these scenes.

238. Geiringer, Karl. "Gluck und Haydn." *Festschrift Otto Deutsch zum 80. Geburtstag*, ed. Walter Gerstenberg, Jan LaRue, Wolfgang Rehm. Kassel: Bärenreiter, 1963, pp. 75–81. ML55 D5 G5.

Attempts to establish the extent to which Gluck and Haydn knew each other and the possibilities of cross-influence. Compares texts and plots of operas set by both composers; concludes that Haydn was familiar with reform ideas but lacked the deep commitment to opera seria to respond fully to these influences.

239. Georges, Horst. *Das Klangsymbol des Todes im dramatischen Werk Mozarts. Studien über ein klangsymbolisches Problem und seine musik-*

alische Gestaltung durch Bach, Handel, Gluck und Mozart. Munich: Ricke, 1937, reprinted 1969. 228 pp. ML410 M9 G66 1969.

Discusses the practice of creating musical symbols to represent death; argues that the same death symbols recur in the works of Bach, Handel, Gluck, and Mozart.

240. Ginguené, Pierre-Louis. *Notice sur la vie et les ouvrages de Nicolas Piccinni.* Paris: Panckoucke, 1801. 144 pp. ML410 P586.

Biographical study of Piccinni. Contains a contemporary account of the state of the Opera before the 1770s; notes the reform of *tragédie lyrique* effected by Gluck and acknowledges the improvement in performance standards he brought about. Detailed account of the Gluck-Piccinni rivalry from the point of view of a devoted Piccinnist.

241. Gruber, Gernot. "Gluck und Mozart." *Hamburger Jahrbuch für Musikwissenschaft: Die frühdeutsche Oper und ihre Beziehungen zu Italien, England und Frankreich* 5 (1981): 169–186. ISBN 3 9215 1859 8. ML5 H16.

Reviews earlier attempts to compare Gluck and Mozart. Makes a detailed comparison between *Iphigénie en Tauride* and *Die Zauberflöte*, noting the Enlightenment principles underlying both works; referring to Dahlhaus (items 426 and 427) and the Stolls (item 478), investigates the role of music in representing character development in each work, with a detailed comparison of form, phrase-structure, and symmetry in "D'une image, hélas!" (*Iphigénie*, III.1) and "Ach ich fühl's" (*Zauberflöte*, II.4).

242. Heartz, Daniel. "From Garrick to Gluck: the Reform of Theatre and Opera in the Mid-Eighteenth Century." *Proceedings of the Royal Musical Association* 94 (1967–1968): 111–127. ISSN 0080 4452. ML L8 M8.

Investigates the interconnections between the reform of acting technique brought about by David Garrick and Gluck's reform of opera. Deals with the contribution of the Encyclopedists in forming eighteenth-century taste, the innovations of Noverre and Angiolini, and Guadagni's role in effecting a direct link between Garrick and Gluck.

243. Jäger, Erich. "Gluck und Goethe." *Die Musik* 21 (1913–1914): 131–139. ML:5 M9.

Argues that Gluck and Goethe were connected by many common sympathies and documents the points of rapprochement between them.

244. Kirk, Elise K. "Padre Giambattista Martini: Some Little-Known Aspects." *American Music Teacher* June/July (1977): 16–18. ML1 A5.

Assesses Martini's reputation as man and teacher; deduces the warm esteem in which he was held by many eighteenth-century musicians including Gluck. Based on a study of Martini's letters; a useful adjunct to Hortschansky (item 55).

245. Kohut, Adolph. "Wieland und Gluck." *Neue Zeitschrift für Musik* 80/3 (1913): 32–35. ML5 N4.

Traces the support given to Gluck's Paris operas through Wieland's contributions to the *Deutscher Merkur*. Shows how Wieland replied to La Harpe's criticism of *Iphigénie en Aulide*, using extensive quotation from La Harpe. Gives the text of a letter from Wieland to Gluck concerning a proposed collaboration which never took place.

246. Longyear, R. Morgan. "Binary Variants of Early Classic Sonata Form." *Journal of Music Theory* 13/2 (1969): 162–185. ML1 J68.

Analyzes and compares different types of binary structures in the works of C. P. E. Bach, Mozart, D. Scarlatti, Alberti, Rutini, Gluck (the overture to *Alceste*), Filtz, J. C. Bach, Beck, Benda, Haydn, and Vanhal.

247. Marek, Robert Carl. "The Use of Harmonic Patterns of Similar Sonorities in the Music of Gluck, Mozart, Cherubini and Beethoven." Doctoral dissertation, University of Rochester, New York, 1957. 2 vols.

248. Monelle, Raymond. "Gluck and the festa teatrale." *Music & Letters* 54 (1973): 308–325. ISSN 0027 4224. ML5 M64.

Examines the genre of the *festa teatrale* and identifies many of the reform aspects of *L'innocenza giustificata* and *Orfeo* with the conventions of the genre. Compares *Orfeo* with Hasse's *Alcide al bivio* (1760). See also Sternfeld (item 205), Buschmeier (item 375), Degrada (item 429), Martina (item 454), and Joly (item 551).

249. Nagel, Willibald. *Gluck und Mozart.* Langensalza: Beyer und Söhne, 1905. 36 pp. ML55 M7.

Attempts to clarify both the personal relationships between the two composers and the extent of Gluck's influence on Mozart; based on documentary and secondary descriptive sources rather than on the evidence of the music.

250. Nettl, Paul. "Casanova and Music." Trans. Theodore Baker. *The Musical Quarterly* 15 (1929): 212–232. ISSN 0027 4631. ML1 M725.

A study of Casanova's musical contacts, including Gluck, Piccinni, Calzabigi, and Migliavacca, based in part on unpublished documents.

251. Panzacchi, Enric. "Una lotta musicale: Gluk [*sic*] e Piccinni." *Nuova antologia di scienze, lettere ed arti.* Terza serie 97/13 (Jan. 1888): 193–215. AP37 N8.

Criticizes Calzabigi's limitations and credits Gluck with the major role in the reform. Describes Gluck's impact on Paris and especially on Rousseau. Briefly considers Piccinni's career and argues that the Gluck-Piccinni dispute reflected a wider debate current throughout Europe and lasting well into the nineteenth century. Claims that Gluck's influence is discernable in Verdi.

252. Rackwitz, Werner. "Gluck Händel-Beziehung." *Wissenschaftliche Konferenz zu den 26. Handelfestspielen der DDR*, ed. Walther Siegmund-Schulze. Halle: Wissenschaftliche Beiträge, Martin Luther Universität, 1977, pp. 5–24. AS182 H125 1976, 22.

Discusses the thesis that Gluck's reforms were anticipated in the oratorios of Handel. Compares the two composers, inferring a similarity in the way both approached innovation by building on the legacy of existing styles. Compare Baselt (item 220).

253. Ringer, Alexander. "A German Gluckist in Pre-Revolutionary France." *Music in the Classic Period: Essays in Honor of Barry S. Brook*, ed. Allan W. Atlas. New York: Pendragon, 1985, pp. 221–231. ISBN 0 9187 28371. ML195. M87 1985.

Identifies Johann Christoph Vogel as one of Gluck's most devoted followers; traces Gluck's influence in his work; argues that Vogel's opera *Demophon* was one of the harbingers of the French Revolution.

254. Roberts, John H. "The 'sweet song' in *Demofoonte*: a Gluck Borrowing from Handel." *Opera and the Enlightenment*, ed. Thomas Bauman and Marita Petzoldt McClymonds. Cambridge: Cambridge University Press, 1995, pp. 168–188. ISBN 0 521 46172 3. ML 1720.3.063 1995.

Discusses the popular aria "Ogni amante" appearing in a *pasticcio* version of *Demofoonte*, London 1755. Traces how the music, originally a minuet by Handel in *Arianna in Creta* (1734), was used by Gluck as "Se all'impero" (*La clemenza di Tito*), and "Ogni amante" (*Issipile*), both composed in 1752. Notes a further Gluck/Handel borrowing of "Il cor mio" (*Alessandro*, 1726) in *La fausse esclave* (1758).

255. Robinson, Michael. *Opera Before Mozart*. London: Hutchinson, 1966. 168 pp. ISBN 0 09 080421 X. ML1700 R56.

In the course of a study of the conventions and problems of early opera, argues that Gluck's approach succeeds best in the simplest situations, where his ability to characterize in depth can have fullest scope.

256. Rolland, Romain. "Gluck." *Musiciens d'autrefois*. Paris: Hachette, 1906, pp. 203–246. 15th ed., 1949. ML390 R642.

A landmark in early twentieth-century Gluck criticism. Contains two major essays, the first describing Gluck as a reformer and arguing that his reforms were, on every point, anticipated by the Encyclopedists, the second dealing with Gluck's artistic development, from national affiliations to Italian opera, German *Lied* and French opera, towards an international style.

257. ———. "Gluck, une revolution dramatique." *Revue de Paris* 11 (1904): 736–772. AP20 R27.

Draws connections between Gluck's reform and the dramatic theories of the Encyclopedists. Criticizes Rameau (and his champion, Debussy; see Eckart-Baecker, item 306), for outdated attitudes. Argues that the Encyclopedists advocated a triple reform: of performance standards, of librettos, and of musical declamation.

258. Rushton, Julian. "An Early Essay in Leitmotiv: J. B. Lemoyne's *Electra* (1783)." *Music & Letters* 52 (1971): 387–401. ISSN 0027 4224. ML5 M64.

Examines the evidence for Gluck's influence on Lemoyne, who claimed to have inferred his technique of leitmotiv from Gluck's *Iphigénie en Aulide*. See also Garlington (item 175).

259. ———. "The Theory and Practice of Piccinnism." *Proceedings of the Royal Musical Association* 93 (1971–1972): 31–46. ISSN 0080 4452. ML28 L8 M8.

Analyzes differences between Gluck's and Piccinni's dramatic styles. Deals principally with phrasing tempo and modulation in the arias and more briefly with recitative and orchestration. Compares the influence of Gluck and Piccinni in the decades immediately after their deaths.

260. ———. "*Iphigénie en Tauride*: The Operas of Gluck and Piccinni." *Music & Letters* 53 (1972): 411–430. ISSN 0027 4224. ML5 M64.

A comparison of the two operas. Discussion includes dramatic structure, libretto, and characterization. Deals with Gluck's numerous self-borrowings, concluding that his opera "is perhaps the most brilliant pasticcio ever produced." Many music examples from both operas. Compare Hortschansky (item 179).

261. Sadie, Stanley. "Some Operas of 1787." *The Musical Times* 122 (1981): 474–477. ISSN 0027 4666. ML5 M85.

A brief comparative study of operas by Mozart, Gazzaniga, and Salieri; argues that Salieri attempted to pursue Gluckian principles in *Tarare*.

262. Saint-Foix, Georges de. "Les débuts Milanais de Gluck." *Gluck-Jahrbuch* 1 (item 87): 28–46.

Attempts to establish the extent of Gluck's debt to Sammartini in the early operas. Compares Sammartini's *Agrippine* (1742) with *Demofoonte* and *Ipermestra*. Argues that Sammartini's influence is also discernable in trio sonatas and notes the relationship between Gluck's overture to *Le nozze* and a Sammartini symphony. Compare Churgin (item 227).

263. Schnoebelen, Anne. "The Growth of Padre Martini's Library as Revealed in His Correspondence." *Music & Letters* 57 (1976): 379–397. ISSN 0027 4224. ML5 M64.

Notes the formation of a significant eighteenth-century music library; locates Gluck's career in the context of his contemporaries and sheds light on the attitudes of Martini as one his most judicious and informed admirers.

264. Strohm, Reinhard. *Die italienische Oper im 18. Jahrhundert*. Wilhelmshaven: Heinrichshofen, 1979. 404 pp. ISBN 3 7959 01103. ML1703 S87.

Analyzes the changing relationship between drama and music. Argues that innovations in the libretto preceded the musical reforms; examines the dramatic techniques of Arcadia, Zeno, Metastasio, Calzabigi, and Coltellini; distinguishes between music which "clothes the drama" (Scarlatti, Vinci, Hasse) and that which "expresses the drama" (Jommelli, Gluck, Mozart).

265. ———. "Tradition und Fortschritt in der *Opera Seria*." *Christoph Willibald Gluck und die Opernreform* (item 83), pp. 325–352.

Investigates the influence of reform principles on Italian opera in the 1760s. In a wide-ranging discussion of opera seria, assesses the degree of innovation in two works with librettos by Coltellini, Traetta's *Ifigenia in Tauride* and Gluck's *Telemaco*.

266. Surian, Elvidio. "Il mito dell'eroismo e la funzione politica della musica: il *Chant du départ* (1794) di Méhul." *Mitologie. Convivenze di musica e mitologia: testi e studi*, ed. Giovanni Morelli. Venice: La Biennale di Venezia, 1979, pp. 214–224. ML42 V33 F44 1979.

Attempts to relate music and literature to contemporary political situations. Argues that three works, Racine's *Iphigénie en Aulide* (1674), Gluck's *Iphigénie en Aulide* (1774), and, in a more detailed study, Méhul's *Chant du départ* are all connected with phases of French territorial aggression.

267. Vetter, Walther. "Glucks Stellung zur tragédie lyrique und opera comique." *Zeitschrift für Musikwissenschaft* 7 (1924–1925): 321–355. ML5 I68. Reprinted in *Mythos-Melos-Musica* (item 84), vol. 1, pp. 309–326.

Traces stylistic parallels between Rameau and Gluck and examines Gluck's acquisition of French stylistic attitudes in the comic operas. In a detailed commentary on *Iphigénie en Tauride*, shows how Gluck had fully assimilated French influences.

268. ———. "Gluck und seine italienischen Zeitgenossen." *Zeitschrift für Musikwissenschaft* 7 (1924–1925): 609–646. ML5 Z37. Reprinted in *Mythos-Melos-Musica* (item 84), vol. 2, pp. 220–251.

Attempts to determine Gluck's indebtedness to his Italian contemporaries. Traces connections severally between Gluck and Hasse, Jommelli, Davide Perez, Francesco di Majo, and Traetta. Concludes that Jommelli and Traetta most closely approached Gluck's achievements but stresses the wide currency of reform attitudes.

269. ———. "Georg Christoph Wagenseil, ein Vorläufer Christoph Willibald Glucks." *Zeitschrift für Musikwissenschaft* 8 (1926): 385–402. ML5 Z37. Reprinted in *Mythos-Melos-Musica* (item 84), vol. 1, pp. 236–262.

Detailed stylistic comparison between Wagenseil and Gluck, based on Wagenseil's contribution to the *pasticcio Euridice* (1750).

270. ———. "Deutschland und das Formgefühl Italiens." *Deutsches Jahrbuch der Musikwissenschaft* 4 (1959): 7–37. ML5 D479.

Based on Wölfflin's analysis of antitheses between German and Italian culture (see items 212 and 213). In detailed comparisons of Vinci with Jommelli, Caldara with Wagenseil, and Paisiello with Mozart, identifies Gluck as a synthesizer of the contrasting attitudes to form and expression shown by North and South European composers.

271. ———. "Der Opernkomponist Georg Christoph Wagenseil und sein Verhältnis zu Mozart und Gluck." *Hermann-Abert-Gedenkschrift*, ed. Friedrich Blume. Halle: Max Niemeyer, 1928. ML423 A2 V3. Reprinted in *Mythos-Melos-Musica* (item 84), vol. 1, pp. 227–235.

Develops the discussion in item 269. Examines individual aspects of Wagenseil's operatic style and finds specific correspondences between his music and that of Gluck, Mozart, and Beethoven, particularly in his use of the chorus, the short aria, and the treatment of the orchestra.

272. Viertel, Karl-Heinz. "Christoph Willibald Gluck und die Oper seiner Zeit." *Musik und Gesellschaft* 27/10 (1977): 591–597. ML5 9033.

Argues that Gluck's reform did not take place in isolation. Traces parallel Enlightenment trends in the legitimate theater, particularly in the rejection of the hampering influences of Corneille, Racine, and Spanish drama. Points to the changing concept of characterization from types to individuals. Shows how Gluck's operas focused these general trends and suggests that they continued to influence the development of opera up to the time of Wagner.

*Weichlein, William J. "A Comparative Study of Five Settings of Metastasio's libretto *La clemenza di Tito* (1734–1791)." Cited below as item 404.

273. Wellesz, Egon. "Franceso Algarotti und seine Stellung zue Musik." *Sammelbände der Internationalen Musikgesellschaft* 15 (1913–1914): 427–439. ML5 I66.

Establishes the importance of Algarotti's essay (item 1) in all areas of theater reform in the mid-eighteenth century, particularly in his relationship to Gluck.

274. Whittall, Arnold. "Rousseau and the Scope of Opera." *Music & Letters* 45 (1964): 369–376. ISSN 0027 4224. ML5 M64.

Discusses Rousseau's attitudes to music and society advanced in the "Lettre sur la musique française" (item 34). Examines the conflict between Rousseau and Rameau and the alleged parallels between Rousseau and Wagner. Argues that the value of Rousseau's ideas is severely restricted by the inadequacy of his technique, especially his lack of understanding of harmony. Briefly analyzes the unique qualities of the French language.

275. Yorke-Long, Alan. *Music at Court. Four Eighteenth-Century Studies*. London: Weidenfeld & Nicolson, 1954. xviii, 158 pp., reprinted Westport, CT: Hyperion Press, 1979. ISBN 0 88355 770 3. M160 Y6 1979.

Investigates Traetta in Parma, Jommelli in Würtemberg, Hasse in Dresden, and Graun in Berlin. Discusses in passing the relationship of these composers to Gluck, pinpointing differences of style and personality. Attributes an essential role to Traetta in responding to the current of reform.

3. GLUCK RECEPTION

276. Abert, Hermann. "Die erste Kritik von Glucks Orpheus." *Gluck-Jahrbuch* 2 (item 87): 105–107.

Analyzes the anonymous criticism in the *Wienerisches Diarium* of October 13, 1762 of the first performance of *Orfeo*. Contains complete text of the review and brief commentary.

277. ———. "Über Entstellungen und Parodien Gluckscher Opern." *Gluck-Jahrbuch* 2 (item 87): 108–109.

Editorial footnote to Engländer (item 233). Adds details of various performances of *Orfeo* in the later eighteenth century, and notes deviations from the score of 1762. Mentions three Italian parodies of the opera by Paisiello, Traetta, and Da Capua, and argues that Italian parodies deride Gluck whereas French parodies (see Cucuel, item 304) offer an affectionate tribute.

278. Angermüller, Rudolph. "Kassenschlager Gluck an der Pariser Académie Royale de Musique." *De editione musices: Festschrift Gerhard Croll zum 65. Geburtstag*, ed. Wolfgang Gratzer and Andrea Lindmayr. Laaber: Laaber Verlag, 1992, pp. 109–124. ISBN 3 8900 7263 1. ML55 C83 1992.

Traces Gluck's varying commercial fortunes at the Opera, arguing that for the majority of his productions he was a box-office hit, ensuring the viability of the opera house.

279. Anon. [*"Iphigénie en Aulide."*] *Mercure de France* May (1774): 157–180. AP20 M48.

Detailed review of the opera and its immediate reception. Discusses Gluck's reform principles as expounded in his letter to the *Mercure* in February 1773 (translated in Howard, item 56, pp. 106–107).

280. ———. [*"Orphée."*] *Mercure de France* September (1774): 190–198. AP20 M48.

A comprehensive review of the opera and its performance, warmly favorable to both the poem and the music.

281. ———. [*"Alceste."*] *Mercure de France* May (1776): 166–170; June (1776): 183–184. AP20 M48.

Brief review of the opera, not wholly favorable. Second passage records the alterations to the score following the introduction of Hercules. Compare Mairobert (item 339).

282. ———. [*"Armide."*] *Journal de Paris* 267 (1777): 3–4.

Reviews the first performance. Appreciative of Gluck's style in general but critical of the dramatic weaknesses of the poem. Compare La Harpe (item 334).

283. ———. [*"Armide."*] *Mercure de France* October (1777): 150–154. AP20 M48.

A brief, curiously noncommittal review of the premiere and its reception.

284. ———. [*"Iphigénie en Tauride."*] *Journal de Paris* 139 (1779): 558–559; 154 (1779): 619.

Reviews the first performance. Commends the integrated overture but deplores the introduction of Diana. Notes the exclusion of intrigue ("Nous ne croyons pas inutile de remarquer que le mot amour n'est pas prononcer dans le cours entière des quatres actes") and ballet interludes. Commends the "barbaric" orchestration of the Scythians' dances. The addition of Gossec's ballet finale is noted briefly in the second notice. See also Gastoué (item 437), and La Harpe (item 332).

285. ———. [*"Écho et Narcisse."*] *Journal de Paris* 268 (1779): 1090–1091; 272 (1779): 1106–1107; 222 (1780): 903–904.

Reviews the first performances of *Écho*. Deals mostly with the poem, criticizing its dramatic weaknesses. Warmly appreciative of the music, commending in particular the characterization of the protagonists and the fine choruses. Second notice reports changes to the score but deals mainly with the ballets; commends the designs. Third notice records further changes for the revival in 1780, chiefly cuts in the role of Amour. The *Journal de Paris*'s enthusiastic advocacy of the opera brought many protests. Compare item 286.

286. ———. [*"Écho et Narcisse."*] *Mercure de France* October (1779): 164–172. AP20 M48.

Introduces the opera but comments almost exclusively on the poem. Affirms the continuing validity of myth in the theater but criticizes the librettist's approach to dramatizing such an inherently undramatic story.

287. Antonicek, Theophil. "Beethoven und die Gluck-Tradition." *Festgabe der Österreichischen Akademie der Wissenschaften zum 200. Geburtstag von Ludwig van Beethoven.* Vienna: Böhlau, 1970, pp. 195–220. ISBN 3 2050 3649 2.

Suggests a spiritual affinity between Beethoven and Gluck and shows how Gluck's operas were held to be models for German national opera in the early decades of the nineteenth century.

288. Arcais, Francesco d'. "L'*Orfeo* del Gluck." *Nuova antologia di scienze, lettere ed arti* terzia serie 102/18 (Nov. 1888): 111–123. AP37 N8.

Examines a recent successful revival of *Orfeo* and the taste for "*l'antico*" in late nineteenth-century Italy. Analyzes the conventions of *Orfeo*, dealing with the vocal casting of Orpheus, the extensive ballets, the overture, and the *lieto fine*. Pleads for a better education in understanding eighteenth-century performance practice.

289. Arend, Max. "Der Stil Glucks." *Zur Kunst Glucks* (item 80), pp. 1–30.

Seeks to explain why Gluck's operas have dropped out of the repertory. Analyzes Gluck's expressive vocabulary, including his harmonic resources and use of tonality, in particular the expression of grief in a major key. Discusses the relationship between Gluck and Wagner and argues that Wagner has equipped audiences to understand Gluck.

290. Arnaud, François (abbé). "Lettre de M. l'abbé Arnaud au P. Martini." *Mélanges de littérature* (item 361), vol. 2, pp. 299–310.

Focuses on the debate between Italian and French opera in Paris in the 1770s. Defends Gluck in the Gluckist-Piccinnist dispute, arguing Gluck's superiority over the Italians in word-setting, accompanied recitative, chorus-writing, overtures, and general points of style. See Martini's reply (item 341).

291. ———. "Profession de foi en musique." *Mélanges de littérature* (item 361), vol. 2, pp. 313–321.

Conveys the tone and nature of the arguments surrounding Gluck's reputation in Paris. Attacks La Harpe's championship of Italian opera and praises the dramatic truth of Gluck's works.

292. ———. "La soirée perdue à l'Opéra." *Mélanges de littérature* (item 361), vol. 2, pp. 322–336. Reprinted in Lesure (item 336), vol. 1, pp. 46–61.

Recreates the arguments and atmosphere in Paris in the 1770s; defends Gluck against both Lullist and Piccinnist attacks.

*Bachaumont, Louis Petit de, M. F. Pidansat de Mairobert, Moufle d'Angerville and others, eds. *Mémoires pour servir à l'histoire de la république des lettres en France depuis 1762 jusqu'à nos jours.* Cited as item 5.

*Balleyguier, Delphin. *L'Alceste de Gluck.* Cited as item 417.

293. Berlioz, Hector. *A travers chants.* Paris: Lévy, 1862. 336 pp. ML410 B5 A. Ed. Léon Guichard, Paris: Grund, 1971. 491 pp. ML410 B5 A56. The Gluck essays from this volume, trans. Edwin Evans, appear as *Hector Berlioz: Gluck and his Operas.* London: Reeves, 1915. 167 pp. ML410 B5 A543.

The essays on *Orphée* and *Alceste* arise from the revivals Berlioz directed in Paris in the mid-nineteenth century but transcend their occasional nature by their perceptive and authoritative interpretation of Gluck's dramatic genius. Evidence of both the enormous enthusiasm for the revivals and their economic success.

294. Bertrand, Jean-Edouard-Gustave. *Étude sur l'Alceste de Gluck.* Paris: n.p., 1861. 40 pp. ML550 B47.

Notes the enthusiasm for Gluck in Paris after the Berlioz revival of *Orphée.* Prepares the ground for the revival of *Alceste* with an account of its history and a brief appreciation of its style.

*Bitter, Carl Hermann. *Die Reform der Oper durch Gluck und R. Wagners Kunstwerk der Zukunft.* Cited as item 222.

295. Bouyer, Raymond. "La statue de Gluck, musicien français." *Le ménestrel* 67 (1901): 322–323. ML5 M465.

Argues for an enduring tension between "Gluckist" and "Piccinnist" composers. Claims Mozart and Wagner as Piccinnist and Berlioz, Méhul, Saint-Saëns, and Massenet as Gluckist, and thus claims that Gluck's dramatic theories influenced the principal opera composers in nineteenth-century France.

296. Breunlich, Maria Christine. "Gluck in den Tagenbüchern des Grafen Karl von Zinzendorf." *Gluck in Wien* (item 81), pp. 62–68.

Lists references to Gluck in the unpublished Zinzendorf diaries (Haus-, Hof-, und Staatsarchiv in Vienna), providing valuable evidence for the reception of Gluck's stage works.

297. Bricqueville, Eugène de. *L'Abbé Arnaud et la réforme de l'Opéra au XVIII siècle.* Avignon: Seguin Frères. 1881. 29 pp. ML1727 35 B81.

Defines Arnaud's role in the Gluck-Piccinni controversy. Attributes his immediate sympathy with Gluck's aims to his early classical studies. Describes the artistic circle which supported Gluck between 1774 and 1779 and the varied reception accorded his Paris operas.

298. Brown, Bruce Alan. "*Les rêveries renouvelées des Grecs*: Facture, Function and Performance Practice in a Vaudeville Parody of Gluck's *Iphigénie en Tauride* (1779)." *Timbre und Vaudeville: zur Geschichte und Problematik einer populären Gattung im 17. und 18. Jahrhundert*, ed. Herbert Schneider. Hildesheim: Olms, 1999, pp. 306–343. ISBN 3 487 10934 4.

Discusses parodies of productions at the Comédie Française and the Académie Royale as criticisms of the originals. Investigates a parody of *Iphigénie en Tauride* by Favart that uses material from an earlier parody of the play on which Guillard's libretto was based. Reveals the wide range of cultural references Parisian operagoers brought to their role as audience.

299. Candiani, Rosy. "*L'Alceste* da Vienna a Milano." *Giornale storico della letteratura italiana* 161 (1984): 227–240. ISSN 0017 0496. PQ4001 G5.

Traces the changes made to the *Alceste* libretto by Giuseppe Parini for the production at the Regio Ducal Teatro, Milan, in 1768–1769. Argues that the secondary roles were expanded and much of Calzabigi's intensity lost in the interests of pleasing both the company and the taste of a less attentive audience.

300. Cattelan, Paolo. "Sul gluckismo di Wagner: Un'aggiunta: Lettura incrociata di *Tristan* ed *Iphigénie en Tauride*." *Rassegna veneta di studi musicali* 2/3 (1986): 217–234.

Investigates Wagner's reading of *Iphigénie*; argues that Wagner misunderstood Gluck's and Guillard's unfolding of the myth. Traces parallels between Gluck's operas and *Tristan und Isolde*.

301. Coquéau, Claude-Philibert. *Entretiens sur l'état actuel de l'Opéra de Paris.* Amsterdam and Paris: Esprit, 1779. vi, 174 pp. Reprinted in Lesure (item 336), vol. 2, pp. 267–540.

Piccinnist analysis of Gluck's reputation in Paris. Claims that Gluck's operas won popular acclaim only because the Italian style was little known in France, arguing that wherever the Italian style was known it would always be preferred; detailed attacks on *Iphigénie en Aulide, Alceste, Armide,* and *Iphigénie en Tauride.*

302. Corancez, Olivier de, "Lettre sur le Chevalier Gluck." *Journal de Paris*
     231 (1788): 997–999; 234 (1788): 1009–1011; 237 (1788): 1021–1023.
     Also appears translated into German in *Allgemeine Musik-Zeitung* 14
     (1812). ML5 A43.

     Invaluable eyewitness account of Gluck's reputation in Paris, including his
     relationship with Rousseau. Contains (allegedly) Gluck's own explanations
     of problem passages in his music. One of the earliest sources of many well-
     known anecdotes, including Gluck's much-quoted statement: "avant de tra-
     vailler, mon premier soin est de tâcher d'oublier que je suis musicien."

303. Corri, Domenico. *A Select Collection of the Most Admired Songs, Duetts
     etc. from Operas in the Highest Esteem*. Edinburgh: John Corri, 1779, vol.
     1, 122 pp. M1497 C61.

     Includes decorated versions of three arias from *Orfeo*: "Che farò," "Chi-
     amo il mio ben," and "Deh placatevi con me." The thesis that these ver-
     sions, headed "sung by Signor Guadagni," represent authentic Gluck
     performance practice is controversial. See Neumann (item 192).

304. Cucuel, Georges. "Les operas de Gluck dans les parodies du XVIII siècle."
     La revue musicale 3/5 (1922): 210–221; 3/6 (1922): 51–68. ML5 R613.

     Briefly traces the history of the operatic parody in Paris and surveys paro-
     dies of Gluck's Paris operas. Argues that it was the plots and characters of
     Gluck's operas which were satirized rather than the music, though the style
     of singing he required also came under attack: "Crier est tout, chanter n'est
     rien" (p. 54). See Brown (item 298).

305. Deutsch, Otto Erich. "Aus Schiedenhofens Tagebuch." *Mozart-Jahrbuch*
     (1957): 15–24. ML410 M9 A11.

     Contains entries from the diary of Johann Baptist Schiedenhofen, includ-
     ing an entry for January 19, 1776, referring to a performance in Salzburg of
     Die zwei Königinnen, "by Gluck." Nothing more is known of this probably
     spurious work, and the possibility that it is a confused reference to *Die
     Maienkönigin* (see Arend, item 486, and Schünemann, item 498), has not
     been investigated.

306. Eckart-Baecker, Ursula. "Claude Debussys Verhältnis zu Musikern der
     Vergangenheit." *Die Musikforschung* 30 (1977): 56–63. ISSN 0027 4801.
     ML5 M9437.

     Traces Debussy's pronouncements on past composers (Rameau, Couperin,
     Bach, Gluck) in his writings. Attempts to account for Debussy's antipathy

to Gluck both on political grounds and because of his strong preference for Rameau, with whose operatic concept he saw Gluck as being in conflict. Compare Romain Rolland (item 257).

307. Engländer, Richard. "Gluck und der Norden." *Acta musicologica* 24 (1952): 62–83. ISSN 0001 6241. ML5 I6.

Investigates Gluck's influence in Scandinavia. Lists performances of his works in Copenhagen and Stockholm and traces their influence on the native repertory.

308. "Erzählender, Der." "Glucks Opern in Berlin: oder 'Was ist das?'" *Allgemeine musikalische Zeitung* 20 (1837): 327. ML5 A43.

A curiosity bearing on the reception history of Gluck's works. Attacks the impression given in an earlier number of the same journal (8 (1837): 127) that all Berlin was seized with a great enthusiasm for Gluck as a result of the revival of *Armide*. Replied to by Schmidt (item 352).

309. Fauquet, Joël-Marie. "Berlioz's version of Gluck's *Orphée*." *Berlioz Studies*, ed. Peter Bloom. Cambridge: Cambridge University Press, 1992, pp. 189–253. ISBN 0521 41286 2. ML410 B5 B363.

Major study of Berlioz's version of *Orfeo/Orphée*. Traces the performance history of *Orphée* at the Opera prior to 1859 and notes Berlioz's critical response to the work in these decades. Reviews the source material, including Berlioz's annotations of the Vienna and Paris scores, and a range of manuscript material. Lists Berlioz's modifications of both text and music, including an appendix presenting two versions of the vocal line of the title role, one published by Berlioz in 1859, the other by Viardot Garcia in 1872. Argues that Berlioz initiated the Gluck revival in the nineteenth century, both rediscovering the almost forgotten score of 1762 and securing a permanent place for *Orphée* in the repertory.

310. Forkel, Johann Nicolaus. "Schreiben, woraus ein Componist lernen kann, auf welche Weise man der Direktoren der Académie royale de Musique in Paris Lust zu einer neuen Oper machen müsse." *Musikalischer Almanach für Deutschland* 4 (1789): 151–163. ML20 M63.

Satirical response to Du Roullet's letter to the directors of the Opera (Lesure, item 336, vol. 1, pp. 1–10) and Chabanon's letter to the *Mercure de France* (translated in Mueller von Asow, item 61, pp. 35–44) on the suitability of the French language for opera.

311. ———. [Review of "Briefe über die Wienerische Schaubühne" by Joseph Kurzboch.] *Allgemeine deutsche Bibliothek* 10/2 (1769): 28–32. Partly reprinted in *Musikalische-kritische-Bibliothek*. Gotha: C. W. Ettinger, 1778, vol. 1, pp. 174–176. ML4 M31.

An attack on *Alceste* in response to early adulatory criticism. Claims *Alceste* has too much music to make good declamation and too little music to be considered an opera.

312. ———. [Review of the score of *Alceste*.] *Allgemeine deutsche Bibliothek* 14/1 (1771): 3–27. Reprinted in *Musikalische-kritische-Bibliothek*. Gotha: C. W. Ettinger, 1778, vol. 1, pp. 176–199. ML4 M31.

Trenchant critical discussion of the preface and of Gluck's aims, particularly those which reduce the role of music. Analyzes the nature of musical expression. Attacks instances of "poverty of invention" in the music.

313. ———. [Review of the score of *Paride ed Elena*.] *Allgemeine deusche Bibliothek: Anhang zu den 13–24*. Baden (1777): 481–486. Reprinted in *Musikalische-kritische-Bibliothek*. Gotha: C. W. Ettinger, 1778, vol. 1, pp. 200–206. ML4 M31.

Continues the criticism in item 312, attacking Gluck's aims and in particular his "misuse" of declamation.

314. Friebe, Freimut. " 'Che farò' bei George Eliot und John Galsworthy: der englische Gentleman und die musik im 19. Jahrhundert." *Christoph Willibald Gluck und die Opernreform* (item 83), pp. 237–254.

Examines references to "Che farò" in novels by George Eliot and John Galsworthy and infers a cultural awakening in nineteenth-century England. Argues that while both authors identified the aria as a symbol of heartfelt emotion, the power of the music was less well understood by Eliot's mid-nineteenth-century readers than by Galsworthy's readers half a century later.

315. Fuller-Maitland, J. A. "Der Streit um die dramatische Wahrheit in der Oper." *Gluck-Jahrbuch* 1 (item 87): 86–90.

Discusses the changing concepts of music drama from the Florentine Camerata to Richard Strauss, and Gluck's pivotal role between Monteverdi and Wagner. Identifies a permanent tension between dramatic truth and entertainment value in opera, of which the changing role of closed forms is symptomatic.

316. Geiringer, Karl. "Hector Berlioz und Glucks Wiener Opern." *Gluck in Wien* (item 81), pp. 166–170.

Gives an overview of Berlioz's reception of Gluck's Viennese operas on the evidence of quotations in his *Traité d'instrumentation*, his revisions of *Orfeo* and *Alceste* for Paris, and his critical writing in the *Gazette musicale*.

317. Gerber, Rudolf. "Wege zu einer neuen Gluck-Betrachtung." *Die Musik* 34/4 (1941–1942): 89–98. ML5 M9.

Surveys changes in the perception and understanding of the nature of Gluck's genius in the eighteenth to twentieth centuries. Argues against the overemphasis in early twentieth-century criticism (for example Abert, items 155 and 157) on Gluck's "rationalist" approach, and examines many eighteenth-century sources in an attempt to reestablish Gluck as an expressive composer inspired by an innate feeling for nature rather than by acquired dramatic theory.

318. Gevaert, François-Auguste. *Cours méthodique d'orchestration*. Paris: Lemoine, 1890. 331 pp. MT70 G37.

Based on Berlioz (item 162). Extensive quotation from Gluck's scores: the number of Gluck quotes is exceeded only by those from Beethoven and Mendelssohn. Evidence of Gluck's standing among composers in the late nineteenth century.

319. Glasenapp, Carl Friedrich. "Gluck." *Wagner-Enzyklopädie*. Leipzig: Fritzsch, 1891, vol. 1, pp. 217–227. ML410 W1 A145.

Gathers the major references to Gluck in Wagner's writings into four short essays: the reform, the overture, performance, Gluck and Mozart. Full sources of all extracts given. A convenient starting point for research, but see Wagner editor Kapp (item 364).

320. Goldschmidt, Hugo. *Die Musikästhetik des 18. Jahrhunderts und ihre Beziehung zu seinem Kunstschaffen*. Zurich: Rascher, 1915, reprinted Hildesheim: Olms, 1968. 461 pp. ML3845 G65 1968.

A comprehensive study examining the basis of aesthetic and polemical literature in the eighteenth century. Part II, pp. 263–450, is devoted to opera and centers on Gluck's works and the development of eighteenth-century opera criticism.

321. Grimm, Friedrich Melchior. *Correspondence littéraire, philosophique et critique*. Paris: Buisson, 1813. 3rd· ed., Paris: Garnier Frères, 1877–1882. 16 vols. PQ773 G7 1877.

Valuable primary source giving detailed reviews of the premieres of all Gluck's Paris operas, subsequent revisions, their reception, insights into performance practice, and accounts of some of the polemical literature surrounding Gluck. See also Kretzschmar (item 328).

322. Grossegger, Elisabeth. *Theater, Feste und Feiern zur Zeit Maria Theresias, 1742–1776, nach den Tagebucheintragungen des Fürsten Johann Joseph Khevenhüller-Metsch.* Vienna: Österreichische Akademie der Wissenschaften, 1987. xii, 433 pp. ISBN 3 7001 0800 1. AS142 V31 Bd. 476.

Excerpts the entries from Khevenhüller-Metsch (item 24) that apply to the theaters and other entertainments.

323. Hass, Robert. "Von dem Wienerischen Geschmack in der Musik." *Festschrift Johannes Biehle zum sechzigsten Geburtstage*, ed. Erich Hermann Müller von Azow. Leipzig: n.p., 1930, pp. 59–65.

Reproduces an anonymous article published in the *Wienerisches Diarium* on October 18, 1766, and analyzes it as evidence of Gluck's reputation in Vienna immediately after *Orfeo*. Heartz attributes authorship to Ditters (item 119).

324. Heckmann, Herbert. *Das Problem der Identität: E. T. A. Hoffmann. Ritter Gluck.* Berlin: Mayer, 1997. 112 pp. ISBN 3 93238 6080 6. PT2360 R53 H43 1997.

Analyzes Hoffmann (item 326); argues that Hoffmann imaginatively identified with Gluck, whom he saw as an icon of the Romantic artist.

325. Henzel, Christoph. "Zwischen Hofoper und Nationaltheater: Aspekte der Gluckrezeption in Berlin um 1800." *Archiv für Musikwissenschaft* 50/3 (1993): 210–216. ISSN 0003 9292. ML5 A63.

Traces the performance history of Gluck's operas in Berlin at the close of the eighteenth century. While most productions were given as concert performances, the staging of *Iphigenie auf Tauris* in 1795 made a vital contribution to the establishment of the Nationaltheater in Berlin, creating a demand for German opera and provoking a debate on opera aesthetics. See also Reichardt (item 347).

326. Hoffmann, Ernst Theodor Wilhelm. *Ritter Gluck. Eine Erinnerung aus dem Jahre 1809. Allgemeine Musik-Zeitung* 11 (1808–1809): cols. 305–319. ML5 A43.

A fantasy account of a meeting with the ghost of Gluck. Evidence of the romanticizing of Gluck at the turn of the century. Notes in passing some abuses in performance practice, including playing the overture to *Iphigénie en Aulide* before a performance of *Iphigénie en Tauride*. Discussed in Heckmann (item 324).

327. Kantner, Leopold M. "I teatri viennesi al tempo di Maria Teresa: Tendenze stilistiche nella musica teatrale a Vienna." *Napoli e il teatro musicale in Europa tra Sette e Ottocento: Studi in onore di Friedrich Lippmann*, ed. Bianca Maria Antolini and Wolfgang Witzenmann. Florence: Olschki, 1993, pp. 45–53. ISBN 8 822 24026 X. ML1720. N36.

Analyzes the taste of the Habsburgs and its effect on the opera composers under their patronage. Argues that Gluck, Hasse, Grétry, and Salieri were all subjected to the same influences but reacted to them differently.

328. Kretzschmar, Hermann. "Die Correspondence littéraire als musikgechichtliche Quelle." *Jahrbuch der Musikbibliothek Peters* 10 (1903): 79–92. ML5 J15.

Useful commentary on Grimm (item 321). Assesses the scope and function of Grimm's *Correspondance littéraire*, examines his prejudices against *tragédie lyrique* and his attack on the management of the Académie Royale. Traces Grimm's initial antipathy to Gluck's Paris operas and his eventual capitulation to *Iphigénie en Tauride*.

329. ———. "Für und gegen die Oper." *Jahrbuch der Musikbibliothek Peters* 20 (1913): 59–70. ML5 J15.

Wide-ranging essay discussing eighteenth-century opera criticism. Argues that Marcello (item 27) avoided identifying the real problems of opera while satirizing superficial faults. Contends that Arteaga (item 4) and Algarotti (item 1) were both more judicious and more influential. Claims a role for Ballad Opera and *Singspiel* in transforming opera.

330. Kunze, Stefan. "Christoph Willibald Gluck, oder: die 'Natur' des musikalischen dramas." *Christoph Willibald Gluck und die Opernreform* (item 83), pp. 390–418.

Major Gluck reception study. Traces the growth of enthusiasm for his work among his contemporaries and attributes major roles to Hoffmann (item 326) and Schubart (item 354) in establishing his reputation while identifying the myths on which his reputation was built. Explores the wide currency of the central ideas of the reform among his contemporaries, noting the paradox of a reformer who consistently reused material from his earliest operas and who left unchallenged the conventional "happy ending."

Concludes that Gluck's true reform lay in his role as director and that the aim of performances should be to rediscover his unwritten intentions.

331. La Harpe, Jean-François de. "Réponse de M. de la Harpe à l'Anonyme de Vaugirard." *Journal de politique et de littérature* November 5, 1777. Reprinted in Lesure (item 336), vol. 1, pp. 323–349.

The most detailed of La Harpe's replies to Suard (item 360). Attacks Suard's definition of *"chant"* and *"mélodie"* by citing articles from the *Encyclopédie* (see Rousseau, *Dictionnaire*, item 35). Claims that Gluck's melodies lack the balanced phrasing and self-sufficient structure of Italian airs.

332. ———. *Correspondance littéraire.* Paris: Migneret, 1801. 2nd ed., 1804–1807. 6 vols. PQ273 L3.

Contains many references to the Gluckist-Piccinnist rivalry and reviews of performances; analyzes some of the polemical literature and offers evidence for and against Gluck's musical standing in Paris. Contains the anecdote of Rousseau's final surrender to Gluck: "Puis-qu'on peut, disait-il, avoir un si grand plaisir pendant deux heures, je conçois que la vie peut être bonne à quelque chose" (vol. 1, p. 25).

333. ———. "Über das Gluckische Singspiel *Iphigenia in Aulis.*" *Der Teutsche Merkur* (1776): 260–264. Reprinted in *Musikalische-kritische-Bibliothek.* Gotha: C. W. Ettinger, 1778, vol. 1, pp. 206–210. ML4 M31.

Review of Paris production, attributed to La Harpe and translated by Forkel. Lucid exposition of Gluck's aims related to both Italian and French traditions, with a balanced criticism of the opera. Deals harshly with its weakness but acknowledges many fine passages. Some discussion of the nature of musical expression.

334. ———. [*"Armide."*] *Journal de Politique et de Littérature* October 5, 1777. Reprinted in Lesure (item 336), vol. 1, pp. 259–270.

Reviews the first performance of *Armide.* Gives a detailed account of audience reaction; finds the opera disappointing after *Orphée.* Extensive discussion of Gluck's melodic and declamatory style. Compare items 282 and 283.

335. Le Blond, Gaspard Michel. *Mémoires pour servir à l'histoire de la revolution operée dans la musique par M. le chevalier Gluck.* Paris: Bailly, 1781, 481 pp., reprinted as vol. 1 of Lesure (item 336). Trans. J. G. Siegmeyer as *Ueber den Ritter Gluck und seine Werke.* Berlin: n.p., 1823. viii, 384 pp. 2nd ed., Berlin: Voss'sche Buchhandlung, 1837.

Major documentary source containing the principal articles and letters about Gluck published in the Parisian press between 1772 and 1780. Reviewed in Lesure (item 336), vol. 2, pp. 541–555. Many documents cited separately.

336. Lesure, François. *Querelle des Gluckistes et des Piccinnistes.* Geneva: Minkoff, 1984. 2 vols. ISBN 2 8266 0861 4.

Important facsimile edition of contemporary documents, with brief introduction and commentary. Vol. 1 reproduces Le Blond (item 335). Vol. 2 contains fourteen further documents, of which the most important are cited separately.

337. Liszt, Franz. "Orpheus von Gluck." *Neue Zeitschrift für Musik* 40/18 (1854): 189–192. ML5 N4.

Written on the occasion of the performance at Weimar in February 1854. Chief interest lies in the authorship of the article and the impact this opera had on Liszt's own work. Contains a sensitive discussion of Gluck's dramatic treatment of the myth. Describes the growing importance of declamation in eighteenth-century opera and identifies Gluck as preparing the way for Romantic opera. Compares Gluck's dramatic declamation with that of Schubert, Weber, Spontini, Méhul, and Grétry.

338. Lockspeiser, Edward. "The Berlioz-Strauss Treatise on Instrumentation." *Music & Letters* 50 (1969): 37–44. ISSN 0027 4224. ML5 M64.

Discusses Strauss's revision of Berlioz (item 162). Points up Berlioz's admiration for specific orchestral effects in Gluck's operas and shows how Strauss sought to match if not to displace these with examples from Wagner.

339. Mairobert, Mathieu François Pidansat de. "Lettre XIV, Sur l'Opéra." *L'observateur anglois.* London: Adamson, 1777–1778, vol. 3, pp. 210–237.

Describes the impact of the first performance of *Alceste* in Paris. Includes a description of the theater, its administration, architecture, decoration, and acoustics. Detailed criticism of principal singers and dancers. Compare item 281.

340. Marmontel, Jean-François. *Essai sur les revolutions de la musique en France.* Paris: Académie Française 1777. 60 pp. ML1704 A2 M35. Reprinted in Lesure (item 336), vol. 1, pp. 153–190, with footnote commentary by Le Blond refuting the arguments.

Lengthy essay on the reception of Gluck by rival supporters of French and Italian opera in Paris. Sustained criticism of Gluck for his lack of Italian lyricism and the absence of extended arias in his operas. Commends, however, Gluck's impact on performance standards and recognizes that his style is a hybrid, with German taste predominating. Reviewed in Lesure (item 336), vol. 1, pp. 194–196.

341. Martini, Giovanni Battista. "Réponse du Padre Martini." *Mélanges de littérature* (item 361), vol. 2, pp. 311–312.

Extract from Martini's response to Arnaud (item 290). Accepts Arnaud's argument and commends Gluck's union of Italian and French opera styles with German instrumental style. Claims, however, that Italian singers dislike singing Gluck as his music gives them little opportunity to display their voices.

342. Meylan, Pierre. "Berlioz et la poésie." *Revue musicale de la Suisse romande* 31/3 (1978): 120–126. ML5 R64.

Comments on Berlioz's writings on the relationship between poetry and music and his discussion of Gluck's dramatic theories propounded in the preface to *Alceste*.

343. Nohl, Ludwig. *Gluck und Wagner*. Munich: Finsterlin, 1870. vii, 368 pp. ML1729 4 N8.

Argues that German national opera is music drama—that it began with Gluck and reached fulfillment in Wagner. A rambling and diffuse account full of interesting comparisons but marred by a narrow, nationalistic outlook.

344. Oliver, Alfred Richard. *The Encyclopedists as Critics of Music*. New York: Columbia University Press, 1947. viii, 227 pp. ML1727 04.

Analyzes a wide spectrum of eighteenth-century criticism. Argues (with Rolland, item 257) the importance of the Encyclopedists in initiating and guiding the reform movement in opera. Useful appendices list all the articles on music in the *Encyclopédie* and the authorities on music quoted by the Encyclopedists.

345. Reichardt, Johann Friedrich. "Siebenter Brief." *Vertraute Briefe aus Paris geschrieben*. Hamburg: Hoffman, 1804, vol. 1, pp. 177–215. ML270 R34.

Reviews performances of *Iphigénie en Aulide* and *Alceste* given in Paris in 1802 with added ballets. Discusses the possibility of cutting the opening of the *Iphigénie* overture.

346. ———. "Etwas über Gluck und dessen Armide." *Berlinische musikalische Zeitung* 1 (1805): 109–112. ML5 B45.

Deals with Gluck's reception of Lully, containing a brief account of the Querelle des Bouffons and of how Gluck came to write *Armide*. Reviews the opera appreciatively.

347. ———. "Etwas über Glucks *Iphigenia in Tauris* und dessen *Armide*." *Berlinische musikalische Zeitung* 2 (1806): 57–60. ML5 B45.

Reviews the two operas on the occasion of their performance in Berlin, with some observations on performance practice.

348. Rousseau, Jean-Jacques. "Fragments d'observations sur l'*Alceste* italien de M. le chevalier Gluck." *Traités sur la musique*. Geneva: n.p., 1781, pp. 392–427. ML60 R86.

An analysis of *Alceste*; criticizes the dramatic construction, in particular the lack of action, but is basically sympathetic towards Gluck's treatment. Reiterates his theories of musical expression.

349. ———. "Extrait d'une réponse du petit faiseur à son prête-nom, sur un morceau de l'Orpheé de M. le chevalier Gluck." *Traités sur la musique*. Geneva: n.p., 1781, pp. 428–437. ML60 R86.

Discusses the harmonic content of *Orpheé* Act II, Scene 1, and analyzes the nature of the enharmonic notation of the B natural/C-flat at the Furies' "No!"

350. S., M. [*"Iphigénie en Tauride."*] *Mercure de France* May (1779): 194–201; June (1779): 50–60, 172–180. AP20 M48.

The first entry reviews the premiere, enthusing over both the work and its performance. The second entry gives a detailed account of the poem and records the continuing success of the work in the theater. The third entry notes the addition of a ballet finale by Gossec. Compare item 284.

351. Saint-Saëns, Camille. "La musique de Gluck." *Le ménestrel* 21 (1908): 164. ML5 M466.

A spirited defence of Gluck. Attacks current performance conventions and describes productions seen by the young Berlioz which still preserved the authentic tempos, vigor, and action of performances directed by Gluck.

352. Schmidt, J. P. "Die Frage des Erzählenden: 'Was ist das?' oder: Was ist eigentlich jetzt Berlins Hauptgeschmack?" *Allgemeine musikalische Zeitung* 23 (1837): 379. ML5 A43.

Responds to "Der Erzählender" (item 308). Contends that in Berlin opinion is divided between adherents of serious classical opera and light French Romantic opera and that accordingly only half the city can be said

to be of the Gluck party. Evidence of the tendency of Gluck's music to po-
larize audiences and to inspire factions even after his death.

353. Schollum, Robert. "Grétry-Salieri-Schubert." *Schubert-Kongress Wien 1978.*
Bericht, ed. Otto Brusatti. Graz: Akademische Druck-und-Verlagsanstalt,
1979, pp. 363–371. ISBN 3 210 01103 7. ML410 S3 S2994 1978.

Argues that some aspects of Schubert's melodic style, in particular his
declamation and respect for the text, show the influence of Gluck, transmitted to Schubert through Grétry and Salieri.

354. Schubart, Christian Friedrich Daniel. "Gluk." [*sic*] *Ideen zu einer Ästhetik
der Tonkunst. Allgemeine musikalische Zeitung* 17 (1804): cols. 227–229.
ML5 A43.

Brief assessment of Gluck as a composer who belonged to no school and
who had no successors. Despite factual inaccuracies, gives valuable evidence of how Gluck's achievements were perceived by his contemporaries.
Refutes Forkel's criticisms (item 174), and praises in particular *Hermanns-
Schlacht*, which Schubart heard performed by the composer. Refers to and
amplifies Riedel (item 140).

355. Schuré Edouard. "Gluck créateur du drame musical." *Le drame musical.*
Paris: Sandoz et Fischbacker, 1875. 12th ed., Paris: Perrin, 1914, vol. 1,
pp. 324–343. ML1700 S386.

Typical of panoramic studies of opera evolution in later nineteenth century: makes Gluck the pivotal point of a study of opera from the Florentine
Camerata to Wagner. Dismisses all Gluck's operas before *Orfeo*; claims
Iphigénie en Tauride as his masterpiece. Argues that there is a direct line of
influence from Gluck to Wagner.

356. Sonnenfels, Joseph von. "Nach der zweiten Vorstellung der *Iphigenie in
Tauris*." *Deutsches Museum*. Leipzig: Weygand, May (1782): 400–416.
AP30 D54.

Detailed and sharply critical review of the performance of Alxinger's German translation of the opera given in Vienna in 1781. Comparisons with the
Paris production of 1779 yield useful details of stage design and movement.

357. ———. "Briefe über die Wienerische Schaubühne." *Gesammelte
Schriften*. Vienna: n.p., 1784, vol. 5, pp. 131–392; vol. 6, pp. 1–437.
IB1783 S6.

In a long series of articles criticizing the contemporary theater in Vienna,
Sonnenfels includes an account of the first performances of *Alceste* (vol. 5,

pp. 150–188). Deals with both the work and its performance and reception; acknowledges Gluck's role in creating an international style in opera.

358. Spazier, Johann Carl Gottlieb. *Etwas über Gluckische Musik und die Oper "Iphigénie en Tauris" auf dem Berlinischen Nationaltheater.* Berlin: n.p., 1795. 40 pp.

Near-contemporary discussion of Gluck's style. Includes an examination of his standing in France and a refutation of Handel's judgment on his contrapuntal ability. Concludes with a largely descriptive account of *Iphigénie en Tauride.*

359. Stein, Rudolph G. "Gluck im kritischen Lichte der Zeitgenossen." *Allgemeine deutsche Musikzeitung* 34 (1907): 705–706. ML5 A43.

A collection of short, contemporary responses to Gluck from Handel, Burney, Votaire, Klopstock, Wieland, Herder, Goethe, and Schiller.

360. Suard, Jean Baptiste Antoine. "Lettres de l'Anonyme de Vaugirard." *Journal de Paris* March-November 1777. Reprinted in Lesure (item 336), vol. 1, pp. 115–117, 125–152, 282–313, 354–374.

Series of eight letters chiefly defending Gluck from attacks by La Harpe. Makes detailed and specific replies to criticisms but asserts rather than argues Gluck's superiority over Italian composers. Supporting Gluck's melodic style, Suard emphasizes that Gluck's airs and recitatives make their full effect only in their dramatic contexts. Replied to by La Harpe (item 331).

361. ———. *Mélanges de littérature.* Paris: Dentu, 1803–1804. 2nd ed., 1806. 5 vols. PQ139 S8 1806.

Anthology of source documents by Suard and his contemporaries in support of Gluck, particularly in response to criticism from La Harpe (items 331–334) and Marmontel (item 340).

362. Trampus, Antonio. "Dalla storia delle idee alla storia della musica: Il diario del conte Zinzendorf come fonte per una ricerca interdisciplinare." *Ricercare: Rivista per lo studio e la pratica della musica antica* 5 (1993): 153–169. ISSN 1120 5741.

Discusses Zinzendorf's opinions on opera and communication. Zinzendorf defended the ethical role of tragedy and argued that in order for it to be more easily understood by the audience, the language of tragedy should be closer to colloquial speech and dramatic music should avoid counterpoint.

Appreciated Gluck as an effective communicator, mentioning the German revision of *Iphigenie auf Tauris*.

363. Vismes, Alphonse Denis Marie de. *Lettre à Madame de ***, sur l'opéra d'Iphigénie en Aulide*. Lausanne: n.p., 1774. 23 pp. Reprinted in Lesure (item 336), vol. 2, pp. 9–27. Trans. into German in Riedel (item 140).

A contemporary response to *Iphigénie en Aulide*; testimony to the reverence still accorded Lully at this time. Useful source for the study of Parisian attitudes to Gluck's operas.

364. Wagner, Richard. *Richard Wagners Gesammelte Schriften*, ed. Julius Kapp. Leipzig: Hesse und Becker, 1914. 14 vols. ML410 W1 A1 1914.

Characterizes Gluck as Wagner's forerunner (vol. 1, p. 220; vol. 7, p. 8) and as a reformer (vol. 10, p. 129; vol. 11, pp. 27–29; vol. 12, pp. 234–235). Extended discussion of *Iphigénie en Aulide*, including the translation of the libretto into German (vol. 9, pp. 68–97), the revision of the overture (passing references at vol. 7, pp. 126–127 and 133–134 and full discussion at vol. 9, pp. 98–109). Discussion of *Orfeo* at vol. 13, pp. 147–148. See also Glasenapp (item 319).

365. Wangermann, Ernst. "Wien und seine Kultur zur Zeit Glucks." *Gluck in Wien* (item 81), pp. 13–20.

Argues that it is necessary to be familiar with the cultural climate in mid-eighteenth-century Vienna in order to understand the reception of Gluck's operas there. Deals in particular with the development of German-language theater, identifying Gluck's German version of *Iphigenie auf Tauris* as a landmark.

366. Winternitz, Emmanuel. "A Hommage of Piccinni to Gluck." *Studies in Eighteenth-Century Music. A Tribute to Karl Geiringer on His Seventieth Birthday*, ed. H. C. Robbins Landon. London: Allen & Unwin, 1970, pp. 397–400. ISBN 004 780016 X. ML55 G24 S8.

Provides the text of a letter from Piccinni to the editors of the *Calendrier musical universal pour l'an 1789*, written on the occasion of Gluck's death: a moving tribute, proposing the institution of the annual concert in Gluck's memory.

367. Wörner, Karl. "Die Pflege Glucks an der Berliner Oper von 1795–1841." *Zeitschrift für Musikwissenschaft* 13 (1930–1931): 206–216. ML5 Z37.

A study in reception history. Traces the stage history of Gluck's operas in Berlin from the noteworthy production of *Iphigénie en Tauride* in 1795, the first tragic opera to be given by German singers in Berlin. Demonstrates a steady interest in Gluck's reform operas, especially *Iphigénie en Tauride* and *Armide*, during these years. Attributes a revival of interest in Greek classical drama in Berlin in the 1840s to the stimulus of Gluck's works. Notes the practice of giving the operas with newly composed ballets. See also "Der Erzählender" (item 308), Henzel (item 325), Reichardt (item 347), Schmidt (item 352), and Spazier (item 358).

VI
Specialized Studies
of Individual Works and Genres

1. ITALIAN OPERAS

368. Abert, Hermann. "*Zu Glucks Ippolito.*" *Gluck-Jahrbuch* 1 (item 87): 47–53.

Discusses new evidence concerning the production of *Ippolito* in Milan in 1745, the engraving of Caterina Aschieri in the role of Arsinoe, the view of the stage set, and the text of the aria "Non so placar," missing in Wotquenne (item 49).

369. ———. "Glucks italienische Opern bis zum Orfeo." *Gluck-Jahrbuch* 2 (item 87): 1–25.

Divides the pre-*Orfeo* operas into those up to *Le nozze* and those from *La Semiramide* to *Antigono*. Argues that those of the earlier group are strongly influenced by Sammartini (see Saint-Foix, item 262) but those of the second group, showing the influence of Hasse, share many dramatic qualities with the reform operas.

370. Arend, Max. "Unbekannte Werke Glucks." *Die Musik* 14/2 (1914–1915): 171–174. ML5 M9.

Describes discoveries of an aria from *Artaserse* (published in item 371), an aria from *Demetrio*, noting its similarity to "I Know That My Redeemer Liveth" (*Messiah*), an aria from *La Sofonisba,* and the unattributed aria "Pace Amor." Gives locations of many hitherto unknown librettos, including those for *Paride, Alceste, Ipermestra, La finta schiava, Poro, Orfeo, Tigrane, Iphigenie auf Tauris* (1781), and *Le nozze*.

371. ———. "Glucks erste Oper Artaxerxes." *Neue Zeitschrift für Musik* 82 (1915): 201–202. ML5 N4.

     Discusses the extent fragments and argues that they confirm the judgment reported in Reichardt's anecdotes (item 139) that the work contains early signs of Gluck's dramatic genius. Draws some comparisons with the Iphigenia operas. The aria "Mi scacci sdegnato" is printed between pp. 208–209.

372. ———. "Das vollständige Textbuch zu Glucks Tigrane." *Die Stimme* 10 (1915–1916): 130–132.

     Describes the discovery of a second copy of the libretto of *Tigrane*, containing the pages that were missing from the copy discussed by Piovano (item 400). Lists the full contents of the opera.

373. Barclay Squire, William. "Gluck's London Operas." *The Musical Quarterly* 1 (1915): 397–409. ISSN 0027 4631. ML1 M725.

     Useful background to the two London operas *La caduta de'giganti* and *Artamene*: gives brief biography of the librettist Francesco Vanneschi; establishes the contents of both operas (with reference to Piovano, item 400), and cites many sources from the contemporary press.

374. Buschmeier, Gabriele. "*Ezio* in Prag und Wien: Bemerkungen zu den beiden Fassungen von Glucks *Ezio*." *Gluck in Wien* (item 81), pp. 85–88.

     Compares the versions of *Ezio* given in Prague in 1749 and Vienna in 1763 and argues, with detailed reference to significant passages, that the revised version shows that Gluck was fully aware of the innovatory steps he had taken in *Orfeo* and that his aim in reworking *Ezio* was to breathe new life into the Metastasian genre while accepting the limitations of its framework.

375. ———. "Opéra-ballet oder festa teatrale? Einige Bemerkungen zu Funktion und Form der Chöre und Ballette in Glucks *Le feste d'Apollo*." *Studien zur Musikgeschichte: eine Festschrift für Ludwig Finscher*, ed. Annegrit Laubenthal. Kassel: Bärenreiter, 1995, pp. 280–288. ISBN 3 7618 1222 1. ML55 F49 1995.

     Argues the genre of *Le feste d'Apollo* is problematic, blending elements of French opera and ballet with Italian pastoral and opera seria; concludes that just as the work marked the union of the Habsburg and Bourbon families, so the work unites Italian and French traditions: French elements include the homage prologue and the growing importance of chorus and ballet throughout the three acts (most fully integrated in *Orfeo*); the Italian tradition is evident in the aria-recitative structure and the use of the castrato voice. Notes that this was the first occasion on which Gluck demonstrated his reform ideals outside Vienna. See also Mecarelli (item 457) and Ulm (item 483), though these deal almost exclusively with the *Atto d'Orfeo*.

376. Croll, Gerhard. "Glucks Debut am Burgtheater. *Semiramide riconosciuta* als Festoper für die Wiedereröffnung des Wiener Burgtheaters 1748." *Österreichische Musikzeitschrift* 31 (1976): 194–202. ISSN 0029 9316. ML5 01983.

An account of the festive reopening of the Burgtheater in 1748 which featured Gluck's opera. Argues that this opera already displayed some reform tendencies.

377. ———. "Eine premiere nach 222 Jahren: Zur Aufführung von Metastasio-Glucks *La Corona* im Schloss Schönbrunn." *Österreichische Musikzeitschrift* 62 (1987): 498–503. ISSN 0029 9316. ML5 01983.

Traces the genesis of the *azione teatrale* intended for performance by the four archduchesses who gave *Il Parnaso confuso* in January 1765. Designed to be performed on the emperor's name day, October 4, the work was cancelled due to the sudden death of the emperor. See Hortschansky (item 389).

378. Dahms, Sibylle. "Glucks Serenata *Le nozze d'Ercole e d'Ebe* und das Gastspiel der Mingotti-Truppe in Dresden und Pilnitz." *Die italienische Oper in Dresden von Johann Adolf Hasse bis Francesco Morlacchi*, ed. Günther Stephan and Hans John. Dresden: n.p., 1988, pp. 439–449. ISSN 0005 8106.

Traces the circumstances of the first performance of *Le nozze* in 1747, noting the collaboration between Gluck and Noverre, Gaetano Vestris, and Maria Vestris.

379. Deutsch, Otto Erich. "Gluck im Redoutensaal." *Österreichische Musikzeitschrift* 21/10 (1966): 521–525. ISSN 0029 9316. ML5 01983.

Commentary on one of five pictures painted on the occasion of the marriage of Joseph II in October 1760, depicting the festal first performance of *Tetide*.

380. ———. "Höfische Theaterbilder aus Schönbrunn." *Österreichische Musikzeitschrift* 22/10 (1967): 577–584. ISSN 0029 9316. ML5 01983.

Describes two paintings representing a performance of *Il Parnaso confuso* given on January 24, 1765.

381. Einstein, Alfred. "Gluck's *La vestale*." *The Monthly Musical Record* 66 (1936): 151–152. ML5 M6.

Relates the discovery of the libretto of *La vestale* (1768), a revision of *L'innocenza giustificata* (1755). Argues that the earlier work played a crucial part in shaping the reform.

382. Engländer, Richard. "Glucks *Cinesi* und *Orfano*." *Gluck-Jahrbuch* 1 (item 87): 54–81.

Examines the fashion for Chinese operas in Vienna.

383. Ferand, Ernst. "Gluck in Laxenburg. Ein vergessenes Pastorale und Ballet." *Zeitschrift für Musik* 105 (1938): 253–259. ML5 N4.

Commentary on *La danza*, noting earlier settings of the libretto. Describes the farewell scenes of the opera as Gluck's personal farewell to the rococo. Suggests that *Alessandro* would serve as a suitable opening ballet.

384. Fürstenau, Moritz. "Das Festspiel *Il Parnaso confuso* von Gluck." *Berliner Musik-Zeitung Echo* 19 (1869): 205–208. ML5 B42.

An account of the first performance in 1765 and the part it played in the family celebrations at the marriage of Joseph II and Maria Josepha.

385. Geiringer, Karl. "Zu Glucks Oper *Il Telemaco*." *Bericht über den Internationalen Musikwissenschaftlichen Kongress Bonn 1970*, ed. Carl Dahlhaus and others. Kassel: Bärenreiter, 1972, pp. 400–402. ML36 I6277.

Corrects misapprehensions over the opera: the libretto is not identical with one set by a Scarlatti and the work does not end with a tragic arioso. Argues that the opera finished with a ballet, probably using music from *Orfeo* (but see Lederer, item 517). Characterizes the opera as a treasure box from which each of Gluck's last operas borrows. Compare Hortschansky (item 179).

386. Gugler, Bernhard. "Urform einer Nummer in Glucks *Orpheus*." *Leipziger allgemeine musikalische Zeitung* 11 (1876): 516–524. ML5 A43.

An analytical account, with many music quotations, of the original version in *Ezio* of the aria which was to become "Che puro ciel" in *Orfeo*.

387. Haas, Robert. "Zwei Arien aus Glucks *Poro*." *Mozart-Jahrbuch* 3. (1929): 307–330. ML410 M9 A11.

Describes the Kieswetter collection in the Wiener Hofbibliothek containing two arias from *Poro* (noted by Liebeskind in item 49). Complete musical text given on pp. 317–330. Briefly discusses other Gluck arias from the same collection which have been adapted to sacred texts.

388. Hortschansky, Klaus. "Gluck and Lampugnani in Italien. Zum Pasticcio *Arsace*." *Analecta musicologica* 3 (1966): 49–64. ISSN 0585 6086. ML160 S893.

Examines the evidence for and against Gluck's participation in the performance of Lampugnani's *pasticcio Arsace* in Milan 1743 and casts doubts on Piovano's attribution of eight arias to Gluck. See Piovano (item 400).

389. ———. "Die Festaufführung fand nicht statt. Bemerkung zu Christoph Willibald Glucks *La corona* (1765)." *Neue Zeitschrift für Musik* 129 (1968): 270–274. ML5 N4.

Describes the tradition of music-making in the imperial family. Establishes the circumstances for which the serenata *La corona* was composed and why it was never performed. See Croll (item 377).

390. ———. "Unbekannate Aufführungsberichte zu Glucks Opern der Jahre 1748 bis 1765." *Jahrbuch des Staatliches Institutes für Musikforschung Preussischer Kulturbesitz 1969* (1970): 19–37.

Presents hitherto unknown reviews of performances of *La Semiramide riconosciuta* (1748), *L'innocenza giustificata* (1775), *Il re pastore* (1756), *La fausse esclave* (1758), *L'île de Merlin* (1758), *La Cythère assiégée* (1759), *Il Parnaso confuso* (1765), *Telemaco* (1765), and *Semiramis* (1765). The criticisms are by Metastasio, van Swieten, and an anonymous correspondent to the *Journal encyclopédique*; argues that these represent three typical attitudes to Gluck: mild scepticism, total rejection, and uncritical enthusiasm.

391. ———. "*Arianna*: ein Pasticcio von Gluck." *Die Musikforschung* 24 (1971): 407–411. ISSN 0027 4801. ML5 M9437.

Investigates Gluck's missing *pasticcio* of 1762, based on the libretto and its preface by Giovanni Battista Migliavacca.

392. ———. "Gluck nella *Gazetta di Milano* 1742–1745." Trans. Roberto Frontini. *Nuova rivista musicale italiana* 6/4 (1972): 512–525. ML5 R66.

Reproduces notices from the *Gazetta* which concern the performances of Gluck's early operas in Milan and Crema. Establishes the correct dates of the first and last performances of *Demofoonte, Tigrane, Arsace*, and *Ippolito* and the first performance of *La Sofonisba*. Notes evidence of

Gluck's growing reputation in Milan and sheds light on some of his collaborators in the theater. Gives the partial text of a previously unknown aria from *Ippolito.*

393. ———. "Unbekanntes aus Glucks *Poro* (1744)." *Die Musikforschung* 27 (1974): 460–464. ISSN 0027 4801. ML5 M9437.

Summarizes current knowledge of Gluck's early works and describes the discovery of the overture, the duet "Se mai turbo" and three arias ("Se viver non poss'io," "Di rendermi la calma," and "Son confusa") from *Poro.*

394. Joly, Jacques. "Deux fêtes théatrales de Métastase: *Le cinesi* et *L'isola disabitata.*" *Chigiana* (item 86): 415–463.

Detailed study of two Metastasian libretti.

395. Kraeft, Kay Kathleen. "Gluck's *Le cinesi*: A Study for Performance." Doctoral dissertation, University of Indiana, 1977. 275 pp.

Contains the full score in a new performing edition with production notes.

396. Kurth, Ernst. "Die Jugendopern Glucks bis *Orfeo.*" *Studien zur Musikwissenschaft* 1 (1913): 193–277. ML55 S9.

In-depth study of the pre-*Orfeo* operas. Examines in turn the recitative, arias, ensembles, treatment of the voice, overtures, orchestration, and texture.

397. Leopold, Silke. "Glucks 'Chinesinnen.'" *Geschichte und Dramaturgie des Operneinakters,* ed. Winfried Kirsch and Sieghart Döhring. Laaber: Laaber Verlag, 1991, pp. 75–81. ISBN 3 8900 7260 7. ML1700 G395 1991.

Argues that the genre of *festa teatrale* allowed composers and librettists greater freedom than did opera seria; claims that in *Le cinesi,* Gluck and Metastasio took advantage of this to combine elements of tragedy, comedy, and pastoral, paving the way for the more extended mixed-genre elements in *Orfeo.* See also Monelle (item 248), Buschmeier (item 375), Degrada (item 429), Martina (item 454), and Joly (item 551).

398. Loppert, Max. "Gluck's Chinese Ladies: An Introduction." *The Musical Times* 125 (1984): 321–325. ISSN 0027 4666. ML5 M85.

A well-documentated account examining the circumstances surrounding the creation of *Le cinesi.*

399. Mondolfi, Anna Bossarelli. "Gluck ed i contemporanei attraverso i mano-scritti donati da Maria Caroline alla città di Napoli." *Chigiana* (item 87): 585–592.

    Account of manuscript copies of *Orfeo, Telemaco, La corona,* and *Il Parnaso confuso* (two versions) in I-Nc.

400. Piovano, Francesco. "Un opéra inconnu de Gluck." *Sammelbände der Internationalen Musikgesellschaft* 9 (1907–1908): 231–281, 448. ML5 I66.

    Describes Piovano's reconstruction of *Il Tigrane,* based on his discovery of the libretto, and his reattribution of arias previously assigned to the spurious *Artamene* (1743). Speculates on Gluck's role in the *pasticcio Arsace* (but see Hortschansky, item 388).

401. Rolland, Romain. "Une œuvre inédite de Gluck." *La revue musicale* 3 (1903): 40–47. ML5 R613.

    Brief account of a newly discovered manuscript copy of *La danza.* Commends Gluck's Italianate melodic fluency; argues that he might be called "the finest Italian composer of his time"; includes the text of the aria "Che chiedi, che brammi?" (pp. 42–47).

402. Tiersot, Julien. "Les premiers operas de Gluck." *Gluck-Jahrbuch* 1 (item 87): 9–27.

    Describes the discovery of manuscript sources for Gluck's first ten operas in F-Pn.

403. Vetter, Walther. "Gluck's Entwicklung zum Opernreformator." *Archiv für Musikwissenschaft* 6 (1924): 165–219. ISSN 0003 9292. ML5 A628. Reprinted in *Mythos-Melos-Musica,* item 84, vol. 2, pp. 180–219.

    Argues that the heart of Gluck's reform lies in his arias. Traces the development of aria technique in the early operas, with many examples from *Ezio* (1750), *La clemenza di Tito* (1752), and *Il re pastore* (1756). Analyzes the use of expressive devices of coloratura, syncopation, asymmetric phrasing, and harmonic color in comparison with Hasse's school and discusses his representation of psychological truth. Concludes that the seeds of reform appear in Gluck's handling of dramatically motivated and strongly characterized arias.

404. Weichlein, William J. "A Comparative Study of Five Settings of Metastasio's Libretto *La clemenza di Tito* (1734–1791)." Doctoral dissertation, University of Michigan, 1956. 518 pp.

    Includes a study of Gluck's opera (1752).

2. REFORM OPERAS

405. Abert, Anna Amalie. "Der Geschmackswandel auf der Opernbühne am Alkestis-Stoff dargestellt." *Die Musikforschung* 6 (1953): 214–235. ISSN 0027 4801. ML5 M9437.

Discusses changing attitudes to opera as reflected in different treatments of the Alcestis story, from the earliest operatic setting by Ziani in 1660 to Wellesz's opera in 1924. Argues that Gluck's version is the most "timeless" interpretation of Euripides's drama.

406. ———. "Ist der Ritter Gluck Freiwild? Zur Stuttgarter Aufführung der *Alceste*." *Neue Zeitschrift für Musik* 124 (1963): 221–222. ML5 N4.

Develops points made by Hermann Abert in item 408, describing a revival of the opera in Stuttgart which cut the happy ending. Argues strongly against the "modernization" of older works and defends Gluck's dramatic concept, with its related needs for closed numbers and closed drama, against a desire to create a spurious relevance for a contemporary audience.

407. ———. "Die Bedeutung der *Opera Seria* für Gluck und Mozart." *Mozart-Jahrbuch* 1971–1972 (1973): 68–75. ML410 M9 A11.

Analyzes the importance of the genre of opera seria in the careers of Gluck and Mozart. Argues that both composers first won acceptance in Italy with the seria genre and that while Gluck, in *Orfeo*, sought consciously to reform the genre, in *Idomeneo*, Mozart sought reform unconsciously.

408. Abert, Hermann. "Glucks *Alkestis* im Stuttgarter Landestheater." *Zeitschrift für Musikwissenschaft* 6 (1923–1924): 353–361. ML5 Z37.

Assesses *Alceste* in the theater, arguing in favor of the Italian version. Discusses Gluck's position in opera history in terms of the tension between poetry and music in the eighteenth century. Claims that the simplicity and consistency of the motivation of the character make *Alceste* a rationalist opera.

409. Allroggen, Gerhard. "La scena degli Elisi nell'*Orfeo*." *Chigiana* (item 86): 369–382.

Traces the relationship of the accompagnato "Che puro ciel" to the earlier versions in *Ezio* and *Antigono*. Discusses the analyses by Kurth (item 396), and Brück (item 421). Identifies a different expressive purpose in each dramatic context and traces Gluck's stylistic development through the three settings.

410. Arend, Max. "Die Ouverture zu Glucks *Paris und Helena.*" *Musikalisches Wochenblatt,* 1905, and *Die Musik,* 1906. Reprinted in *Zur Kunst Glucks* (item 80), pp. 59–71.

Analysis of the overture, showing its thematic connections with the opera. Brief review of editions of the opera available in 1905–1906.

411. ———. "*Paris und Helena* von Gluck." Kunstwart, 1905. Reprinted in *Zur Kunst Glucks* (item 80), pp. 72–76.

Analyzes the opera in terms of both its external events and its inner psychological drama. Compares its exploration of the emotions in a claustrophobic relationship with a similar exploration in *Tristan.*

412. ———. "Die Münchener Bearbeitung des Gluck'schen *Orpheus* aus dem Jahre 1773." *Musikalisches Wochenblatt,* 1909. Reprinted in *Zur Kunst Glucks* (item 80), pp. 77–91.

A detailed account of the revision of *Orfeo* for Munich. See also Engländer (item 233), Fürstenau (item 434), and Cattelan (item 565).

413. ———. "Die unter Glucks Mitwirkung hergestellte, verschollene älteste deutsche Übersetzung der *Iphigenie auf Tauris.*" *Zeitschrift der Internationalen Musikgesellschaft* 7 (1906): 261–267. Reprinted in *Zur Kunst Glucks* (item 80), pp. 92–106.

Discusses the German translation made collaboratively by Gluck and Alxinger for the Vienna performance of 1781. Describes the discovery of an incomplete autograph score with the German text with vocal line in the Petersbibliothek in Leipzig. Closely analyzes the word-settings of this new source in comparison with Alxinger's own translation (published in *Sämtliche Schriften*, Vienna, 1812) and Sander's translation for the Berlin performance in 1795.

414. ———. "Glucks *Orpheus.*" *Almanach für die musikalische Welt,* 1914. Reprinted in *Zur Kunst Glucks* (item 80), pp. 232–241.

Dealing with style and interpretation, discusses Gluck's concept of the title role, describing the dramatic impact of various vocal registers and arguing that today the tenor communicates a similar intensity to the castrato in the eighteenth century: argues strongly, therefore, for the French version of the opera.

415. Armellini, Mario. *Le due Armide: metamorfosi estetiche e drammaturgiche da Lully a Gluck.* Turin: De Sono, 1991. 326 pp. ISBN 3 680 1927. ML1727 A75 1991.

Compares Lully's and Gluck's settings; attributes the differences to the different responses by each composer to the aesthetic of his age; discusses the attitudes of the Encyclopedists to Lullian *tragédie*, and the role of the Querelle des Bouffons in bringing about change. Detailed analysis of the two monologues "Enfin il est en ma puissance" (II.5) and "Le perfide Renaud me fuit" (V.5). See also Buschmeier (item 422).

416. Baethge, Wilhelm. "Die Opernreform Christoph Willibald Glucks als Ausdruck einer sich andernden Geisteshaltung im 18. Jahrhundert." *Wissenschaften und Musik unter dem Einfluss einer sich andernden Geisteshaltung*, ed. Manfred Büttner. Bochum: Brockmeyer, 1992, pp. 77–85. ISBN 3 8916 0039 6. BD175 G44 1992.

Argues that a shift in Gluck's depiction of the gods, from benevolent powers to capricious despots, reflects a change in the intellectual environment under the Enlightenment. Argues that the alterations made by Gluck and Du Roullet in creating the French *Alceste* transform the drama from a conflict between humans to a conflict between men and gods.

417. Balleyguier, Delphin. *L'Alceste de Gluck*. Paris: Tresse, 1861. 16 pp.

Brief stage history of the French version from 1776 to 1861. Contains quotations from satirical literature prompted by the controversy surrounding the first performances in Paris.

418. Ballola, Giovanni Carli. *"Paride ed Elena." Chigiana* (item 86): 465–472.

Argues that the part played by *Paride* in the reform differs from that of *Orfeo* and *Alceste*. Identifies its significance as developing Gluck's portrayal of the sensuous and the ironic, comparing this with Mozart's in *Così fan tutte*. Concludes that *Paride* is a unique work, superficially more traditional than the earlier reform operas but nonetheless influential for the future course of opera.

419. Beghelli, Marco. "Le bugie di Oreste." *Christoph Willibald Gluck nel 200 anniversario della morte* (item 82), pp. 435–445.

Discusses, in the context of Orestes's soliloquy, "Le calme rentre dans mon cœur," Hanslick's arguments on the limitations of musical expression. Argues that throughout the opera Gluck's music is tightly bound up with the words and succeeds in being continuously expressive.

420. Brown, Bruce Alan. "Durazzo, Duni, and the Frontispiece to *Orfeo ed Euridice*." *Studies in Eighteenth-Century Culture* 19 (1989): 71–97. ISSN 0360 2370. CB411 S8.

Traces the publication history of the frontispiece to the first published score; argues that Durazzo's choice of an engraving, based on a vignette from an *opéra-comique*, deliberately underlined the common ground between *Orfeo* and *opéra-comique*.

421. Brück, Paul. "Glucks *Orpheus.*" *Archiv für Musikwissenschaft* 7 (1925): 436–476. ISSN 0003 9292. ML5 A63.

Critical comparison of the versions of 1762 and 1774. Useful for its examination of the differences brought about by the change from Italian to French word-setting.

422. Buschmeier, Gabriele. "Glucks *Armide* Monolog: Lully und die 'Philosophes.'" *Festschrift Klaus Hortschansky zum 60. Geburtstag*, ed. Axel Beer. Tutzing: Schneider, 1995, pp. 167–180. ISBN 3 7952 0822 X. ML55 H646 1995.

A comparison between Lully's and Gluck's settings of the monologue "Enfin il est en ma puissance" (II.5). Argues that the two settings reveal differing attitudes to expression: Lully, representing the values of the court, emphasized regularity and restraint; Gluck, in the climate of sensibility, emphasized the passions. Compare Armellini (item 415).

423. ———. "'... de l'emploi du mètre ... dépend le grand effet de l'expression musicale': Du Roullet, Gluck und die Prosodie." *Festschrift Christoph-Hellmut Mahling zum 65. Geburtstag*, ed. Axel Beer, Kristina Pfarr, Wolfgang Ruf. Tutzing: Schneider, 1997, pp. 203–210. ISBN 3 7952 0900 5. ML55 M23 1997.

Argues that Du Roullet, in *Iphigénie en Aulide*, effected a reform of the libretto, breaking with the scenic and metrical structures used by Quinault. Evaluates Du Roullet's commentary in *Lettre sur les drames-opéra* (item 20) with his practice in *Iphigénie* and assesses how far Gluck's unconventional setting departed from the metrical units provided by his librettist. Compare Angermüller (item 541).

424. Croll, Gerhard. "Glucks *Alceste* in Wien und Paris." *Österreichische Musikzeitschrift* 48/5 (1993): 231–236. ISSN 0029 9316. ML5 01983.

Places the Italian *Alceste* at the heart of Gluck's reform of opera seria. Compares the Italian and French versions in terms of performance environment and reception, noting the changes to the libretto, particularly the introduction of Hercules in the French version. Argues that the interpretation of the title role was supremely important for Gluck, who took great pains to train both Bernasconi (1767) and Levasseur (1776) in the role.

425. Cumming, Julie Emelyn. "Gluck's Iphigenia Operas: Sources and Strategies." *Opera and the Enlightenment*, ed. Thomas Bauman and Marita Petzoldt McClymonds. Cambridge: Cambridge University Press, 1995, pp. 217–239. ISBN 0 521 46172 3. ML 1720.3.063 1995.

Sets Gluck's two Iphigenia operas in the context of earlier operatic settings and his own self-borrowings; argues that although both subjects had been chosen by reform composers and *Iphigénie en Aulide* was the ideal subject for opera recommended by Algarotti and Diderot, Gluck fulfilled his dramatic ideals more thoroughly in *Iphigénie en Tauride*, which meets all the requirements of neoclassical opera.

426. Dahlhaus, Carl. "Ethos und Pathos in Glucks *Iphigenie auf Tauris.*" *Die Musikforschung* 27 (1974): 289–300. ISSN 0027 4801. ML5 M9437.

Argues that while "Pathos," or the representation of a single emotional state, is the central concept of baroque opera, "Ethos," or total characterization, is the central concept of classical opera. The concepts are examined in connection with *Iphigénie en Tauride*. Dahlhaus identifies the crucial conflict of the opera as the tension between the affective characterization of Orestes and Thoas, and the new spirit of the age represented in the consistency, simplicity, and spontaneity of Iphigenia. The argument is attacked by the Stolls in item 478, and Dahlhaus replies in item 427.

427. ———. "War Schiller aus Missverständnis 'zu Thränen gerührt'? Eine Erwiderung." *Die Musikforschung* 29 (1976): 72–73. ISSN 0027 4801. ML5 M9437.

Brief response to the Stolls (item 478), who claimed that Schiller misunderstood Gluck's aesthetic premises in *Iphigénie en Tauride*. Aims to show how Gluck and Schiller shared basic dramatic theories although they stressed different aspects.

428. Dalmonte, Rossana. "Ripensando a 'Che farò senza Euridice.'" *Intorno a Massimo Mila: Studi sul teatro e il novecento musicale italiano*, ed. Talia Pecker Berio. Florence: Olschki, 1994, pp. 49–64. ISSN 8 8222 4176 2. ML423 M613 I57 1994.

Tests two different theories of expression against the aria "Che farò." Relates the melodic intervals to the intrinsic expression of the text and argues, with Massimo Mila, that the expressive content of an aria is dependent on the relationship between words and music; refutes Roncaglia's thesis that the aria would retain its expressive character if sung to other words.

429. Degrada, Francesco. "'Danze di eroi' e 'saltarelli di burrattini': vicende dell'*Orfeo* di Gluck." *Il palazzo incantato. Studi sulla tradizione del melodrama dal barocco al romanticismo.* Fiesole: Discanto, 1972, vol. 1, pp. 115–131. ML1700 D43.

Analyzes the dramaturgy of *Orfeo*, in particular the tension between the tragic myth and the conventions of the *festa teatrale*. Argues that the opera reveals a typically Enlightenment view of human nature, and that Gluck chose to replace tragedy with "serene contemplation," the focal center of the work being the scene in the Elysian fields. Briefly reviews subsequent versions of the opera. See also Sternfeld (item 205), Monelle (item 248), Buschmeier (item 375), Leopold (item 397), Martina (item 454), and Joly (item 551).

430. Fend, Michael. "Der Fehlschlag von Glucks *Écho et Narcisse* und die Probleme einer 'musikalischen Ekloge.'" *D'un opéra l'autre: Hommage à Jean Mongrédien,* ed. Jean Gribenski, Marie-Claire Mussat, and Herbert Schneider. Paris: Presses Universitaires de France, 1996, pp. 31–43. ISBN 2 840 50063 9.

Argues that the failure of *Écho et Narcisse* is attributable to a confusion of genres. Both libretto and music conflate psychological realism with pastoral conventions, to the confusion of critics and audiences.

431. Finscher, Ludwig. "Der verstümmelte Orpheus. Über die Urgestalt und die Bearbeitung von Glucks Orfeo." *Neue Zeitschrift für Musik* 124 (1963): 7–10. ML5 N4.

Enumerates many and deplores all of the revisions and adaptations of the 1762 score. An exceptionally perceptive and illuminating discussion of the *lieto fine*.

432. ———. "Gluck und das lieto fine: über ein dramaturgisches Problem der heutigen Gluck-Pflege." *Musica* 18 (1964): 296–301. ML5 M71357.

Discusses some recent productions of Gluck's reform operas and condemns the deformities inflicted on Gluck's final scenes in the majority of cases. Examines the conclusions of *Orfeo*, *Iphigénie en Aulide*, and the two versions of *Alceste* and investigates the dramatic truth of Gluck's reworking of a well-worn convention. Discusses but rejects Weismann's interpretation of *Iphigénie* (item 485).

433. Fürstenau, Moritz. "Über die Schluss-Arie des ersten Aktes aus Glucks französischen *Orpheus*." *Berliner Musik-Zeitung Echo* 19 (1869): 261–263; 269–271. ML5 B42.

An account of the controversy surrounding the authorship of "L'espoir re-
nait das mon âme." See Hammond in item 444, pp. 109–112.

434. ———. "Gluck's *Orpheus* in München 1773." *Monatshefte für Musikgeschichte* 4 (1872): 218–224. ML5 M5.

Examines the version of *Orfeo* performed in Munich in 1773. Contains a
table of numbers comparing this score with the 1762 opera. See also Engländer (item 233), Arend (item 412), and Cattelan (item 565).

435. Gallarati, Paolo. *L' Orfeo ed Euridice di Gluck. Versione Viennese del
1762.* Turin: Giappichelli, 1979. 201 pp. ML410 G5 G33.

Major analytical study of *Orfeo* with appendices in which wider aspects of
eighteenth-century opera are discussed.

436. ———. "La sfida di Armide: Gluck 'pittore' e 'poeta.'" *Musica e storia*
7/2 (1999): 465–487. ISSN 1127 0063. ML5 M7257.

Argues that *Armide* shows a departure from Gluck's previous approaches
to opera. Notes pictorial qualities in Gluck's setting of Quinault's text,
making specific comparisons between Gluck's broadly curving melodic
lines and Hogarth's theory of beauty as discussed by Diderot in item 17.

437. Gastoué, Amadée. "Gossec et Gluck à l'Opéra de Paris: le ballet final de
Iphigénie en Tauride." *Revue de musicologie* 16 (1935): 87–99. ML5 R32.

Investigates Gossec's role at the Opéra and his collaboration with Noverre
in composing ballet movements for a variety of operas. Summarizes the
controversy over the final ballet of *Iphigénie* and gives the evidence for
Gossec being its composer. Describes the eight dances that comprise the
ballet finale.

438. Hastings, Margaret. "Gluck's *Alceste.*" *Music & Letters* 36/1 (1955):
41–54. ISSN 0027 4224. ML5 M64.

Examines variants in the source material of the French *Alceste* and describes the early stage history of the work in Paris.

439. Hayes, Jeremy. "*Armide*: Gluck's Most French Opera?" *The Musical Times*
123 (1982): 408–410. ISSN 0027 4666. ML5 M85.

An account of the genesis of *Armide*. Relates the opera to French theater
traditions, especially with regard to spectacle, divertissements, and the importance accorded to recitative.

440. Heartz, Daniel. "*Orfeo ed Euridice*. Some Criticisms, Revisions and Stage-Realizations during Gluck's Life-Time." *Chigiana* (item 86): 383–394.

Traces the early history of *Orfeo*, dealing chiefly with the first performances in Vienna, the engraving of the score in Paris (1763–1764), and the performances in Parma and London in 1769–1770.

441. Howard, Patricia. "*Orfeo* and *Orphée*." *The Musical Times* 108 (1967): 892–894. ISSN 0027 4666. ML5 M85.

Analyzes the differences between the two versions and provides a comparative table of numbers. Discusses the differences of mood and characterization in the two versions. See also item 444.

442. ———. "The Two Lives of Gluck's *Alceste*." *The Listener* (February 14, 1974): 217–218. PN6072 L5.

Describes the two versions, with particular emphasis on plot and characterization. Considers the differences inherent in the Italian and French languages and the effect of these differences on the recitative.

443. ———. "Gluck's two *Alcestes*: A Comparison." *The Musical Times* 115 (1974): 642–643. ISSN 0027 4666. ML5 M85.

Argues the superiority of the French version in terms of dramatic structure and characterization. Identifies the "interrupted da capo aria" as one of Gluck's most expressive devices.

444. ———. ed., *C. W. von Gluck:* Orfeo. (Cambridge Opera Handbooks) Cambridge: Cambridge University Press, 1981, 143 pp. ISBN 0 521 22827 1. ML410 G5 C2.

A comprehensive account, in a series designed for the general reader, of *Orfeo* and *Orphée*. Contains chapters on the Orpheus myth in opera, the writing of *Orfeo* and the reworking of the opera as *Orphée,* the stage history of both versions, and Berlioz's revision of 1859. Presents conflicting arguments by John Eliot Gardiner, Tom Hammond, and Charles Mackerras in favor of each of the versions, with a number-by-number comparison of them.

445. ———. "*Armide*: A Forgotten Masterpiece." *Opera* 30(1982): 572–576. ML5 066.

Examines the conjunction of Gluck and the seventeenth-century librettist Quinault and the conflict of baroque and Enlightenment concepts in the work's dramatic structure.

446. ———. "For the English. *Orfeo* in London in 1773: A Reconstruction."
The Musical Times 137 (1996): 13–15. ISSN 0027 4666. ML5 M85.

Investigates Millico's performance of *Orfeo* in London in 1773 and concludes that the press announcements, which promised the opera "as it originally was performed in Vienna" are inaccurate: a version of the score
revised for Parma in 1769 formed the basis of the production.

447. ———. "The Orpheus Myth: The Singing Hero." *About the House* 1/3
(2001): 20–23. ISSN 1471 9010.

Traces the differing versions of the Orpheus myth and its treatment in a variety of dramatic contexts.

448. Joly, Jacques. "*Paride ed Elena* entre galanterie et reform." *Zwischen
Opera Buffa und Melodramma: italienische Oper im 18. und 19. Jahrhundert*, ed. Jürgen Maehder and Jürg Stenzl. Frankfurt am Main, Lang, 1994,
pp. 67–79. ISBN 3 631 41917 1. ML1733. Z95 1994.

Argues that *Paride* signals a return to the *galant* style and constitutes a
backward step after the expressive reform operas *Orfeo* and *Alceste*.
Claims that the libretto includes many Metastasian traits but that it mod-
ernizes the myth into a bourgeois drama. Compare Ballola (item 418).

449. Jullien, Adolphe. *Favart et Gluck. La cour et l'Opéra sous Louis XVI.*
Paris: Didier, 1878, pp. 323–349. ML1727 3 J94.

An account of the publication of the score of *Orfeo* in 1764, based on
Favart's letters. Examines Berlioz's accusation of plagiarism against Phili-
dor. See Brown (item 420).

450. La Laurencie, Lionel de. "*Orphée*" *de Gluck*. Paris: Mellottée, 1934. 349
pp. ML410 G5 L3.

Full-length historical study of the Orpheus scores of 1762 and 1774. Deals
with the genesis of the operas and their stage history in Europe up to the
1920s. Examines the Orpheus myth and its treatment in Greco-roman literature. Argues that *Orphée* holds a unique place in the history of opera as
the oldest opera to speak directly to modern audiences.

451. Loewenberg, Alfred. "Gluck's *Orfeo* on the Stage with Some Notes on
Other Orpheus Operas." *The Musical Quarterly* 26 (1940): 311–339. ISSN
0027 4631. ML1 M725.

Traces the history of settings of the Orpheus story before Gluck. Describes
the stage history of Gluck's opera, giving a fairly detailed account of the

eighteenth-century performances, and an outline sketch of the nineteenth- and twentieth-century productions up to 1939. Includes a brief list of the parodies of *Orfeo*.

452. Loppert, Max. "*Alceste* Reassessed." *Opera* 25 (1974): 675–680. ML5 066.

Compares the Italian and French versions and argues that the French score is more accessible to contemporary taste but points up the many problems in opting for either version in its pure form. Describes a synthesis by Vittorio Gui produced at La Scala Milan in 1972.

453. Mackerras, Charles. "Which *Orfeo*?" *Opera* 23 (1972): 393–397. ML5 066.

Explains how three versions of the opera came into existence: Gluck's two versions and Berlioz's revision of 1859. Argues that only a compromise between the different versions will yield a practical solution in the opera house today. This material is slightly expanded in item 444, pp. 99–105.

454. Martina, Alessandra. *Orfeo—Orphée di Gluck: Storia della trasmissione e della recezione*. Turin: De Sono (Associazione per la musica), 1995. 415 pp. ISBN 368 0268 7.

Indispensable analysis of the various transformations of *Orfeo* from 1762 to Berlioz and beyond. Investigates the reasons behind each reworking and sheds light on reception issues, tracing a history of public taste in the period reviewed. Argues that despite its origins in the *festa teatrale, Orfeo* was quickly perceived, both by the composer and his audiences, as an instrument of reform, and was developed and adapted accordingly. A useful appendix charts the content of various versions.

455. ———. "Gluck: *Orfeo/Orphée*, tradizioni e tradimenti. Il coro come momento centrale del rinnovamento gluckiano." *Musica/Realta* 18/54 (1997): 159–169. ML5 M739.

Argues that the chorus in the Orpheus operas functions as an independent character in the drama. Traces the influence of the chorus in *tragédie lyrique* and attributes the work's popularity to the dramatic and structural importance of the choruses.

456. Mauser, Siegfried. "Musikalische Dramaturgie und Phänomene der Personencharakteristik in Glucks *Orfeo*." *Gluck in Wien* (item 81), pp. 124–130.

A short exploration of Orpheus's divine and human roles, focusing on tonal and metrical structures in Act I, Scene 1. Argues that Gluck's approach to musical characterization presages Wagner's techniques.

457. Mecarelli, Paola. *"Le Feste di Apollo." Conclusione di un impegno riformistico a Parma.* Parma: Battei, 1991. 78 pp.

Sets the performance of the Parma *Orfeo* in the context of a reform movement already existing in Parma, arguing that it may have played a part in influencing Gluck and Calzabigi. Investigates the role of Guillaume du Tillot in reorganizing the theater and promoting reform elements in the years leading up to 1769. See also Ulm (item 483).

458. Müller-Blattau, Joseph. "Gluck und Racine." *Christoph Willibald Gluck und die Opernreform* (item 83), pp. 83–97.

Traces the genesis of *Iphigénie en Aulide* and makes detailed comparisons between Du Roullet's libretto and Racine's play; concludes that Gluck's setting fulfills all the aspirations of the Encyclopedists.

459. Noiray, Michel. "Gluck's Methods of Composition in His French Operas: *Iphigénie en Aulide, Orphée, Iphigénie en Tauride.*" Master's dissertation, University of Oxford, 1979.

Argues that Gluck repeatedly revised *Iphigénie en Aulide* at the request of the directors of the Académie Royale and the public to comply with traditions of French opera and the pleas of singers and dancers to furnish them with attractive opportunities. Noiray examines the sources for all three operas in detail, accounting plausibly for the reasons behind decisions taken during the composition process. Incorporates item 460.

460. ———. "Der Brief Glucks an Guillard." *Christoph Willibald Gluck und die Opernreform* (item 83), pp. 373–389.

Discusses Gluck's detailed instructions for the fashioning of the libretto of *Iphigénie en Tauride* to accommodate the reuse of an aria from *La clemenza di Tito*; argues that Guillard ignored many of Gluck's requirements, destroying the intimate link between words and music; explores the paradox that the most successful arias in *Iphigénie* were based on opera seria material.

461. Paduano, Guido. "La 'costanza' di Orfeo. Sul lieto fine dell'*Orfeo* di Gluck." *Rivista italiana di musicologia* 14/2 (1979): 349–377. ML5 R79.

Major investigation of the Orpheus myth in literature and opera. Argues that the happy ending is not a compromise with convention but a consciously contrived renewal of dramatic unity. Suggests that the ending arises from a new Enlightenment attitude to the universe in which the tension between erotic and ethical values is reconciled and in which the central core is not the individual but the couple.

462. Paumgartner, Bernhard. "Gedenken zur Dramaturgie des Gluckschen *Orfeo.*" *Österreichische Musikzeitscrift* 3/7–8 (1948): 180–184. ISSN 0029 9316. ML5 01983.

Discusses the problem of authenticity in reviving older operas. Argues that without a knowledge of eighteenth-century performance practice, the work will be unable to make its impact on modern audiences. Claims that the opera contains little of the myth's classical origins and is wholly in the spirit of the eighteenth century. Argues against the nineteenth-century tendency to make the work "antique."

463. Petrobelli, Pierluigi. "L'*Alceste* di Calzabigi e Gluck: l'illuminismo e l'opera." *Quadrivium* 12/2 (1971): 279–293. ISSN 0392 1530. ML5 Q23.

Identifies *Alceste* as a landmark in operatic history. Argues that Metastasian opera is unable to portray character. Notes the extent of Gluck's dependence on French opera traditions and on the contributions of Guadagni and Calzabigi. Links Gluck's aims with those of the Encyclopedists.

464. ———. "La concezione drammatico-musicale dell'*Alceste* (1767)." *Gluck in Wien* (item 81), pp. 131–137.

Argues that interest in the preface has prevented due attention being paid to the work itself; investigates how far the opera puts into practice the reform principles announced in the preface. Analyzes musical and dramatic structure in the opening scenes, concentrating on repetition and continuity, tracing formal coherence on both a small and large scale. Compare Sternfeld (item 477).

465. Pozzoli, Barbara Eleonora. *Dell'alma amato oggetto: Gli affetti nell'* Orfeo ed Euridice *di Gluck e Calzabigi.* Milan: Edizioni degli Amici della Scala (Musica e Teatro: Quaderni degli Amici della Scala), 1989. 67 pp. ISBN 88 85843 07 7. ML410 G5 P58 1989.

Attempts to subject Calzabigi's libretto to psychoanalytical and structuralist investigation.

466. Robinson, Michael. "The 1774 S. Carlo version of Gluck's *Orfeo.*" *Chigiana* (item 86): 395–413.

Useful study of the production of *Orfeo* in Naples in 1774, with an examination of the content and the sources of the variants. Appendix with comparative table of numbers performed in Vienna in 1762, London 1770 and 1771, Florence 1771, and Naples 1774. See also Martina (item 454).

467. Rolland, Romain. "Le dernier opéra de Gluck: *Écho et Narcisse*, 1779." *Revue d'histoire et de critique musicales* 3 (1903): 212–215. ML5 R613.

Reviews the publication of the score in the Pelletan edition (see Tiersot, item 481). Argues that Gluck's practice of self-borrowing affected the stylistic unity of the opera.

468. Ronga, Luigi. "Dell'*Ifigenia in Aulide* e dello stile gluckiano." *Rivista musicale italiana* 56 (1954): 160–163. ML5 R66.

Argues that *Iphigénie en Aulide* shows a more flexible approach to the reform ideals than *Orfeo* and *Alceste*, a greater variety of well-characterized protagonists, and a more extensive range of emotional experience and psychological analysis. Advocates a performance style that would allow the dramatic momentum built into the score by Gluck to control the pacing of the opera.

*Rousseau, Jean-Jacques. "Fragments d'observations sur l'*Alceste* italien de M. le chevalier Gluck." *Traités sur la musique.* Cited as item 348.

469. Rushton, Julian, "Music and Drama at the Académie Royale de Musique (Paris) 1774–1789." Doctoral dissertation, University of Oxford, 1969. 362 pp.

Examines the development of French opera towards the end of the end of the eighteenth century. Traces the influence of the Italian idiom on the native tradition. Argues that the rivalry between Gluck and Piccinni stimulated Gluck to produce a more dramatic style.

470. ———. "From Vienna to Paris: Gluck and the French Opera." *Chigiana* (item 86): 283–298.

Describes the impact of Gluck's operas in Paris. Argues that Gluck has already assimilated many French traits into the style of his Viennese reform operas and identifies *Iphigénie en Tauride* as Gluck's most complete fusion of French and Italian styles.

471. ———. "In Defence of the French *Alceste*." *The Musical Times* 122 (1981): 738–740. ISSN 0027 4666. ML5 M85.

Examines changes of structure and detail in two versions and concludes that the Paris score is the more effective in the theater. See also Howard (item 443), and Loppert (item 452).

472. ———. " 'Royal Agamemnon': the two versions of Gluck's *Iphigénie en Aulide.*" *Music and the French Revolution*, ed. Malcolm Boyd. Cambridge: Cambridge University Press, 1992, pp. 15–36. ISBN 0521 40287 5.

Reviews the changes Gluck made for the 1775 revival of *Aulide*, in particular the intervention of Diana. Argues that the revision weakens the revolutionary power of the original score. Criticizes the *Sämtliche Werke* edition of the score for giving precedence to the revised setting. See also Finscher (item 432), and Weismann (item 485).

473. Sachse, Leopold. "Bemerkungen zu Glucks-Inszenierungen." *Gluck-Jahrbuch* 4 (item 87): 91–98.

Argues that Gluck's operas demand just as detailed and devoted an approach to their staging as Wagner's. Discusses some approaches to designing and producing *Iphigénie en Tauride*.

474. Schneider, Frank. "Texte und Kontexte in Glucks *Iphigenie auf Tauris:* Marginalien zur neuen Übersetzung für die Inszenierung an der Komischen Oper Berlin." *Musik und Gesellschaft* 27/10 (1977): 597–601. ML5 M9033.

Introduces a new translation of the libretto and reviews earlier translations from Alxinger onwards, dealing in passing with aspects of Gluck's word-setting.

475. Sondheimer, Robert. "Gluck in Paris." *Zeitschrift für Musikwissenschaft* 5 (1922–1923): 165–175. ML5 Z37.

Places Gluck's Paris operas in the context of contemporary controversies over French and Italian styles. Argues that Gluck's attitude to drama and the relationship between words and music was unique and that it located him in a pivotal position between classical and Romantic opera.

476. Spitta, Philipp. "*Paride ed Elena* des Ranieri de Calsabigi." *Allgemeine musikalische Zeitung* 15 (1880): cols. 657–664; 673–684. ML5 A43.

Detailed study of the poem, tracing its derivation from Ovid and Vergil and comparing it with earlier operatic settings. Argues that Gluck's characterization of Helen, challenged by Rousseau as an anachronism (see Corancez, item 302), is based not on Homer (as Gluck claimed) but on Ovid.

477. Sternfeld, Frederick W. "Expression and Revision in Gluck's *Orfeo* and *Alceste*." *Essays presented to Egon Wellesz*, ed. Jack Westrup. Oxford: Oxford University Press, 1966, pp. 114–129. ML55 W38 W5.

Discusses the relative strengths of the Vienna and Paris versions of *Orfeo* and *Alceste*. Identifies the increased time dimension of the component sections of the opera as a crucial development of the reform operas and tests the revisions in the light of this element.

478. Stoll, Albrecht, and Karin Stoll. "Affekt und Moral. Zu Glucks *Iphigenie auf Tauris*." *Die Musikforschung* 28 (1975): 305–311. ISSN 0027 4801. ML5 M9437.

Refutes Dahlhaus's interpretation (in item 426) by contrasting the attitudes to "Ethos" and "Pathos" in Gluck and Schiller. Argues that although Schiller esteemed *Iphigénie* as an ideal classical tragedy, Gluck's setting was designed to conform to the conservative (baroque) tastes of his aristocratic audiences and has little connection with Enlightenment aesthetics. See Dahlhaus's reply (item 427).

479. Teneo, Martial. "Les chefs-d'œuvre du Chevalier Gluck à l'Opéra de Paris." *Revue d'histoire et de critique musicales* 8 (1908): 109–116. ML5 R613.

Study of Gluck's years in Paris, based on inventories in the Opéra. Establishes some details of stage design through an examination of the accounts; quotes some of Gluck's recommendations to improve the performance and production of *Écho*. Extensive quotation from documents but lacking specific references.

480. Tiersot, Julien. "Étude sur *Orphée* de Gluck." *Le ménestrel* 62 (1896): 273–385. ML5 M465.

An extensive historical and analytical account. Briefly traces earlier settings of the Orpheus myth in opera and outlines the stage history of Gluck's opera in the nineteenth century. Describes manuscript sources and compares the French and Italian versions. Describes Bertoni's opera on the same libretto (1776), establishing its indebtedness to Gluck.

481. ———. "L'ultima opera di Gluck: *Eco e Narciso*." *Rivista musicale italiana* 9 (1902): 264–296. ML5 R66.

Adapted from the preface to the score in the Pelletan edition. Provides detailed background to the composition of *Écho et Narcisse* and its poor reception in Paris. Argues that the work nevertheless gives a valuable insight into aspects of Gluck's dramatic art, particularly its intimacy of expression, not afforded by the earlier operas.

482. Tocchini, Gerardo. *I fratelli d'Orfeo*. Florence: Olschki, 1998. xvi, 367 pp. ISBN 88 222 4683 7. ML410 G5 T65 1998.

Important study that convincingly traces the influence of Freemasonry in *Orfeo*, affecting the plot, the language, the scenic design, and the music. *Iphigénie en Tauride* is subjected to a less detailed investigation. Tocchini's thesis is supported by his revelation of the presence of a great number of Masons in Gluck's circle of friends and colleagues, both in Vienna and in Paris, and his interpretation throws light on Gluck's dealings with them, even accounting for his choice of *Écho et Narcisse* for the text of his last opera.

483. Ulm, Renate. *Glucks Orpheus-Opern.* Frankfurt am Main: Peter Lang (European University Studies, Musicology, Series 36, vol. 70), 1991. ix, 221 pp. ISBN 3 631 42687 9. ML410 G5 U4 1991.

Definitive study of Gluck's adaptation of *Orfeo* for Parma in 1769, comparing selected scenes from the adaptation with the original score (Vienna 1762) and *Orphée* (Paris, 1774). Useful appendix reproduces documents relating to the theater in Parma in 1769.

484. Vetter, Walther. "Stilkritische Bemerkungen zur Arien-melodik in Glucks *Orfeo.*" *Zeitschrift für Musikwissenschaft* 4 (1921–1922): 27–50. ML5 Z37.

A detailed analytical study of the arias in *Orfeo.*

485. Weismann, Wilhelm. "Der Deus ex Machina in Glucks *Iphigenie in Aulis.*" *Deutsches Jahrbuch für Musikwissenschaft* 7 (1962): 7–17.

Analyzes the role of Calchas in the denouement of the drama and argues that the resolution is brought about by Calchas's command of psychology, diplomacy, and observation of nature rather than by supernatural means. Deals with the failure of Gluck's critics to appreciate this rationalization of myth. Examines the changed ending to the revised score. Compare Finscher (item 432), and Rushton (item 472).

3. *OPÉRAS-COMIQUES*

486. Arend, Max. "Ist die Maienkönigin ein echter Gluck?" *Zur Kunst Glucks* (item 80), pp. 185–197.

Discusses the authenticity of the opera which, as *Les amours champêtres*, Wotquenne (item 49) established as a pastiche. Argues that the score associated with Kalbeck's translation contains additional numbers drawn from Gluck's other *opéras-comiques.* See Brown (item 489), and Schünemann (item 498).

487. ———. "Die Ouvertüren zu Glucks *Cythère assiégée.*" *Zeitschrift für Musikwissenschaft* 4 (1921–1922): 94–95. ML5 Z37.

Discusses the two versions of *La Cythère assiégée*, 1759 and 1775. Gives an account of the recent discovery of the 1759 overture and corrects Wotquenne's information (in item 49) about the 1775 overture.

488. Brown, Bruce Alan. "Gluck's *Rencontre imprévue* and Its Revisions." *Journal of the Americal Musicological Society* 36 (1983): 498–518. ISSN 0003 0139. ML27 U5 A83363.

Detailed study of the genesis of Gluck's last *opéra-comique*, dealing in particular with revisions made during rehearsal, inferred from manuscript sources in A-Wn. The revisions, forced upon Gluck by the death of Isabella of Parma, are described in detail.

489. ———. "Christoph Willibald Gluck and *Opéra-Comique* in Vienna, 1754–1764." Doctoral dissertation, University of California, Berkeley, CA, 1986. 992 pp.

Groundbreaking study of the *opéras-comiques* that constructs a full and detailed picture of the French theater in Vienna, including personnel and audiences, and provides an analysis of the repertory, tracing the development of Gluck's style within the genre.

490. ———. "Gluck als Hauskomponist für das französische Theater in Wien." *Gluck in Wien* (item 81), pp. 89–99.

Traces Gluck's employment at the Burgtheater, clarifying the titles under which he was employed; deals briefly with his activity as Director of Academies and Composer of Ballets; throws light on both his contributions to the repertory of existing *opéras-comiques* and his newly composed works in the genre.

491. ———. "*Le mandarin*: An Unknown Gluck Opera?" *The Musical Times* 128 (1987): 619–623. ISSN 0027 4666. ML5 M85.

Investigates a manuscript libretto by Pierre-Louis Moline in F-Pn for a "comédie chinoise . . . mise en musique par . . . Gluck." Argues that the opera was planned as a reworking of *Le cadi dupé* and suggests a date of 1774–1775.

492. Croll, Gerhard. "Neue Quellen zu Musik und Theater in Wien 1758 bis 1763. Ein erster Bericht." *Festschrift Walter Senn zum 70. Geburtstag*, ed. Erich Egg and Ewald Fässler. Munich: Katzbichler, 1975, pp. 8–12. ISBN 2 87397 097 X. ML55 S565 1975.

Reports the enormously important discovery of Philipp Gumpenhuber's manuscript inventory of the repertories of spoken drama, ballet, and *opéra-comique* of the French troupe at the Burgtheater and the German troupe at the Kärntnertortheater. (For a discussion of this source, see Brown, items 489 and 166.)

493. Cucuel, Georges. *Les créateurs de l'opéra-comique français.* Paris: Alcan, 1914. 243 pp. ML1727 3 C9.

Traces the history of *opéra-comique* in the eighteenth century. Argues that Gluck's comic operas became more emotionally satisfying in the 1760s. Suggests that Gluck lacked disciples equally in his serious and in his comic operas because his style was "inimitable."

494. Haas, Robert. *Gluck und Durazzo im Burgtheater. (Die Opéra-Comique in Wien.)* Vienna: Amalthea-Verlag, 1925. 216 pp. ML1723 8 V6 H13.

Well-documented account of the rising influence of comic opera genres in Vienna from 1752.

495. Holzer, Ludmilla. "Die komischen Opern Glucks." *Studien zur Musikwissenschaft* 13 (1926): 3–37. ML55 S9.

Discusses the development of the genre and the extent of Gluck's contribution to different opera genres in Vienna from 1752. Analyzes the forms and styles employed by Gluck.

496. Preibisch, Walter. "Quellenstudien zu Mozarts *Entführung aus dem Serail.* Die Türkenoper Glucks und über Gluck hinaus." *Sammelbände der Internationalen Musikgesellschaft* 10 (1908–1909): 430–476. ML5 I66.

Investigates the sources for Mozart's *Entführung.* Examines the fashion for Turkish themes in the theater from the seventeenth century, drawing comparisons between *Le cadi dupé, La rencontre imprévue,* and *Die Entführung,* and argues that Mozart was indebted to Gluck for his fiery Turkish rhythms and colorful orchestration. See also Würtz (item 216).

497. Schmidt, Dörte. " '*Cythère assiégée, opéra-comique en un acte*': Favart, Gluck, und die Möglichkeiten der Parodie." *Opernkomposition als Prozess,* ed. Werner Breig. Kassel: Bärenreiter, 1996, pp. 31–45. ISBN 3 7618 12949. ML1700.O69 1996.

Suggests that Durazzo devised a series of plays and operas on the subject of Armida to further his promotion of French genres in Vienna. Identifies Favart's libretto for *Cythère* as part of this series. Argues that it can be read as a parody of Lully's *Armide* and traces structures, e.g., the episode of the Crusaders, that appear to have been taken from Quinault's libretto.

498. Schünemann, Georg. "Das angeblich von Gluck komponierte Schäferspiel *Die Maienkönigin.*" *Allgemeine Musik-Zeitung* 39 (1912): 465–466. ML5 A43.

Challenges the authenticity of *Les amours champêtres*, asserting that Gluck arranged and rehearsed the score but did not compose any of it. Identifies the sources of some of the airs. See Arend (item 486).

499. Wirth, Helmut. "Gluck, Haydn und Mozart: drei Entführungs-Opern." *Opernstudien: Anna Amalie Abert zum 65. Geburtstag*, ed. Klaus Hortschansky. Tutzing: Schneider, 1975, pp. 25–35.

Discusses the fashion for Turkish operas in midcentury Vienna, Gluck's development of the *opéra-comique*, and in particular *La recontre imprévue* (1764).

4. VOCAL MUSIC

500. Arend, Max. "Glucks *De profundis*. Eine Analyse und ein Protest." *Zur Kunst Glucks* (item 80), pp. 38–58.

Seeks to defend the work from earlier criticism of mediocrity. Examines the nature of Gluck's stylistic simplicity and argues that to achieve its full effect the work needs to be performed liturgically. Draws textural comparisons with both *Iphigénie* operas. Briefly notes the available editions.

501. Chochlow, Jurig. "Die Oden und Lieder Glucks." *Gluck in Wien* (item 81), pp. 151–157.

Brief overview of Gluck's solo songs. Sets them within the context of Gluck's development as an opera composer and relates them to the second Berlin Song School; includes a useful examination of Gluck's word-setting.

502. Howard, Patricia. "A Note on Gluck's *De profundis*." *The Musical Times* 105 (1964): 352–353. ISSN 0027 4666. ML5 M85.

Argues that the work contains many similarities in the orchestration and choral writing to *Iphigénie en Tauride*.

503. Kretzschmar, Hermann. "Das deutsche Lied im 18. Jahrhundert." *Geschichte des neuen deutsches Liedes*. Leipzig: Breitkopf & Härtel, 1911, vol. 1, pp. 162–342. ML2829 K83.

Wide-ranging study of German song; Gluck's settings of Klopstock are discussed at pp. 167–169. Argues that Gluck's settings were significant for the development of the *Lied* and that they influenced Neefe. See Seiler (item 505).

504. Seiler, Josef. "Gluck als Kirchenkomponist." *Neue Berliner Musikzeitung* 21/50 (1867): 393–395. ML5 N2.

Concise analysis of *De profundis*. Deals with dramatic expression, instru-mention, structure, and tonality.

505. ———. "Über Glucks und einige anderer Compositionen Klopstock'scher Oden." *Neue Berliner Musikzeitung* 22/33–36 (1868): 264, 272–273, 289. ML5 N2.

Short study of Klopstock's Odes and the relationship between Gluck and the poet. Contrasts Gluck's declamatory settings with more lyrical settings by Neefe, contending that Neefe's would be preferred by a mid-nineteenth-century audience.

5. BALLETS

506. Arend, Max. "Das Szenarium zu Glucks Ballet *Don Juan.*" *Neue Zeitschrift für Musik*, 1905. Reprinted in *Zur Kunst Glucks* (item 80), pp. 31–37.

Discusses the paucity of available editions of the ballet. Describes the discov-ery of the scenario in a manuscript in F-Pn and gives a German translation.

507. ———. "Ein wiedergewonnes Meisterwerk Glucks." *Kunstwart* 33 (1920): 278–285. AP30 K85.

Commentary on the ballet *Sémiramis*. Argues that Gluck was able to write as expressively without as with the assistance of words.

508. Bacher, Otto. "Ein Frankfurter Szenar zu Glucks *Don Juan.*" *Zeitschrift für Musikwissenschaft* 7 (1924–1925): 570–574. ML5 Z37.

An account of a newly discovered scenario for *Don Juan* performed in Frankfurt between 1780 and 1790.

509. Brown, Bruce Alan. "*Zéphire et Flore*: A 'Galant' Early Ballet by Angiolini and Gluck." *Opera and the Enlightenment*, ed. Thomas Bauman and Marita Petzoldt McClymonds. Cambridge: Cambridge University Press, 1995, pp. 189–216. ISBN 0 521 46172 3. ML 1720.3.063 1995.

Establishes the attribution of the ballet *Zéphire et Flore* to Gluck and Angi-olini, and assesses its place in the context of their later development as collab-orating composer and choreographer; argues that the tension between *galant* and reformist approaches to the ballet are detectable in this early work.

510. Croll, Gerhard. "Ein unbekanntes tragisches Ballet von Gluck." *Mitteilung der Gesellschaft für Salzburger Landeskunde* 109 (1969): 275–277.

An account of *Iphigénie*, a *ballet-tragique* with choreography by Angiolini, first performed on May 19, 1765 at Laxenburg. Both the score and the scenario are lost but Croll gives two eyewitness accounts.

511. ———. "Glucks *Don Juan* freigesprochen." *Österreichische Musikzeitschrift* 31/1 (1976): 12–15. ISSN 0029 9316. ML5 01983.

Argues that it was not Gluck's *Don Juan* that was responsible for the fire at the Kärntnertortheater on November 3, 1761: *Don Juan* was never performed in the old Kärntnertortheater.

512. Dahms, Sibylle. "Gluck und das 'Ballet en action' in Wien." *Gluck in Wien* (item 81), pp. 100–105.

Traces the development of a new ballet aesthetic from Du Bos to Noverre, drawing parallels with the reform of opera.

513. Gertsman, Lois. "Musical Character Depiction in Gluck's *Don Juan.*" *Dance Chronicle* 1 (1977): 8–21. GV1580 D233.

Compares different versions of the score and the scenario. Describes the music, identifying characterizing rhythmic motifs, and argues that Gluck devised a unified scheme across the full thirty-one-number score.

514. Gruber, Gernot. "I balli pantomimici viennesi di Gluck e lo stile drammatico della sua musica." Trans. Mila Kiefer-Tarlao. *Chigiana* (item 86): 501–512. Revised as "Glucks Tanzdramen und ihre musikalische Dramatik." *Österreichische Musikzeitschrift* 29/1 (1974): 17–24. ISSN 0029 9316. ML5 01983.

Examines the concept of "dramatic music" in ballet and opera. Argues that Gluck's ballets offer an exceptional opportunity to analyze his dramatic style because the absence of words concentrates the expression of the drama in the music: the idiom is not restricted to a conventionally appropriate vocal line and the time scale is tauter. Includes a detailed study of *Don Juan* which Gruber identifies as contributing decisively to the reform.

515. ———. "Bemerkungen zur *Semiramis.*" *Gluck in Wien* (item 81), pp. 106–115.

Compares the structure of Voltaire's drama with Angiolini's scenario; examines Gluck's expressive response to the dramatic situations.

516. Haas, Robert. "Der Wiener Ballet-Pantomime im 18. Jahrhundert und Glucks *Don Juan.*" *Studien zur Musikwissenschaft* 10 (1923): 6–36. ML55 S9.

Defines Angiolini's role in the repertory of the ballet in Vienna, with a particular study of *Don Juan*. Includes Angiolini's preface and scenario in French and German.

517. Lederer, Josef-Horst. " '. . . e con una danza festosa finische lo spettacolo': Bemerkungen zum Schluss von Glucks *Telemaco*." *Gluck in Wien* (item 81), pp. 116–123.

Develops Geiringer's discussion (item 385) on the missing closing ballet. Disagrees with Geiringer's suggestion of a ballet with music taken from *Orfeo*; notes the similarity of the endings of *Ezio* (1763) and *Telemaco* and concludes that the *Ezio* ballet might have been reused. In a postscript acknowledges recent research showing that the ballets for *Ezio* were the work of Gassmann and Angiolini.

518. Russell, Charles C. "The Libertine Reformed: *Don Juan* by Gluck and Angiolini." *Music & Letters* 65/1 (1984): 17–27. ISSN 0027 4224. ML5 M64.

Examines the "explosion" of Don Juan operas and the ballets in the decades immediately following Gluck's work. Argues that Angiolini reinterpreted the subject matter as material for tragedy, endowing Don Juan with the nobility and courage which are absent in earlier versions of the legend.

519. Tozzi, Lorenzo. "Attorno a *Don Juan*." *Chigiana* (item 86): 549–564.

Places the ballet in the context of the reform and relates Angiolini's scenario to other versions of the story. Compares the two versions of the score and identifies passages in which Gluck's dramatic ideals of simplicity, truth, and nature are evident in this score.

520. ———. "*Sémiramis*." *Chigiana* (item 86): 565–570.

Argues that *Sémiramis* has been undeservedly neglected and merits a role in Gluck's œuvre as seminal as that accorded *Don Juan* and *Orfeo*.

6. INSTRUMENTAL MUSIC

521. Churgin, Bathia. "The Symphonies of G. B. Sammartini." Doctoral dissertation, Harvard University, 1963. 888 pp.

See also item 227.

522. Gerber, Rudolf. "Unbekannte Instrumentalwerke von Christoph Willibald Gluck." *Die Musikforschung* 4 (1951): 305–318. ISSN 0027 4801. ML5 M9437.

Examines the sources and authenticity of numerous instrumental works, including three trio sonatas, various sinfonias, and the ballets *Alessandro* and *Achille*. But see LaRue (item 523) for further discussion of the symphonies.

523. LaRue, Jan. "Gluck oder Pseudo-Gluck." *Die Musikforschung* 17 (1964): 272–275. ISSN 0027 4801. ML5 M9437.

Questions the authenticity of the D minor sinfonia discussed by Gerber (item 522). Outlines the problems of conflicting sources in eighteenth-century symphonic works.

524. Lipsius, Ida Maria (La Mara). "Gluck als Symphoniker." *Neue Zeitschrift für Musik* 89/50 (1893): 525–526. ML5 N4.

Refutes the suggestion by Pardall (item 525), that Gluck's instrumental works are unknown. Cites her own research (in item 129) in which she lists all currently known unattributed sinfonias by Gluck.

525. Pardall, H. "Eine Symphonie von Gluck." *Neue Zeitschrift für Musik* 89/31 (1893): 146–147. M15 N4. Revised in *Monatshefte für Musikgeschichte* 25/7 (1983): 113–115. ML5 M5.

Important only in respect of understanding the argument in Lipsius (item 524). Gives an account of a "newly discovered" three movement sinfonia in C. Errs both in failing to compare it with the overtures to *Paride ed Elena* and *La Cythère assiégée* (1775) and in claiming it as Gluck's only unattributed sinfonia. See also Arend (item 487).

VII

Gluck's Collaborators in the Theater

1. CHOREOGRAPHERS

526. Abert, Hermann. "J.G. Noverre und sein Einfluss auf die dramatische Bal-
letkompositionen." *Jahrbuch der Musikbibliothek Peters* 15 (1908):
29–45. Also in *Gesammelte Schriften und Vorträge*, ed. Friedrich Blume.
Halle: Niemayer, 1929, reprinted Tutzing: Schneider, 1968, pp. 264–286.
ML60 A18 1968.

Contextual study of the career of Jean-Georges Noverre, noting particularly his absorption of ideas from the *Encyclopédie* and his influential role
in integrating ballet into plot in French opera.

*Angiolini, Gasparo. *Dissertation sur les ballets pantomimes.* Cited as
item 2.

*———. *Lettere di Gasparo Angiolini a Monsieur Noverre.* Cited as item 3.

527. Derra de Moroda, Friedericka. "The Ballet-Masters Before, at the Time of,
and After Noverre." *Chigiana* (item 86): 473–485.

Argues that far from inventing the *ballet d'action,* Noverre played a com-
paratively minor part in the gradual evolution of a genre first manifest in
the seventeenth century. Outlines the work of Noverre's predecessors and
traces his influence forward into the nineteenth century.

*Dahms, Sibylle. "Glucks Serenata *Le nozze d'Ercole e d'Ebe* und das
Gastspiel der Mingotti-Truppe in Dresden und Pilnitz." Cited as item 378.

*———. "Gluck und das 'Ballet en action' in Wien." Cited as item 512.

528. Haas, Robert. "Der Wiener Bühnentanz von 1740 bis 1767." *Jahrbuch der Musikbibliothek Peters* 44 (1937): 77–93. ML5 J15.

Brief study of the reform of ballet in Vienna. Compares and evaluates the contributions of Hilverding and Angiolini.

529. Krüger, Manfred. *J.-G. Noverre und das "Ballet d'Action."* Emsdetten: Verlag Lechte, 1963. 280 pp., 113 plates.

In-depth analytical study of Noverre's work based on his writing and scenarios. Argues the strength of his continuing influence through to Folkine.

530. Lynham, Deryck. *The Chevalier Noverre, Father of Modern Ballet: a Biography.* London: Sylvan Press, 1950. 204 pp. GV1785 N7 L8.

Biographical study. Summarizes Noverre's *Lettres* (items 31 and 32) and argues the importance of Noverre's knowledge of anatomy as the basis of his reformation of the dance.

*Noverre, Jean-Georges. *Lettres sur la danse et sur les ballets.* Cited as item 31.

*———. *Lettres sur la danse, sur les ballets et les arts.* Cited as item 32.

531. Tozzi, Lorenzo. *Il balletto pantomimo del settecento: Gasparo Angiolini.* L'Aquila: Japadre, 1972, 179 pp. ISBN 88 7006 138 8. GV1785 A67 T69.

Analyzes Angiolini's contribution to the reform of ballet on the basis of both his choreography and his little-known ballet music. Argues that his concept of realistic movement in narrative scenarios has influenced ballet up to the present day.

532. ———. "La poetica angioliniana del balletto pantomimo nei programmi viennesi." *Chigiana* (item 86): 487–500.

Examines Angiolini's theoretical writings and traces the development of his thought between the *Dissertation* (item 2) and his *Lettere . . . a Monsieur Noverre* (item 3). Argues that Angiolini, unlike Noverre, never wanted to pronounce on the theory of ballet reform but wanted only to be a practical exponent of reform ideas.

2. DESIGNERS

533. Decugis, Nicole, and Suzanne Reymond. *Le décor de théâtre en France du moyen age à 1925.* Paris: Compagnie Française des Arts Graphiques, 1953. 197 pp. PN2621 D4.

Useful collection of theater designs with concise commentary. Slodtz's settings for *Armide* (Plate 60) and Belanger's for *Alceste* (Plates 61 and 62) illustrate neoclassical design in the 1770s.

534. Fischer, Carlos. *Les costumes de l'Opéra*. Paris: Librairie de France, 1931. 324 pp. ML1727 8 P2 F4.

Lavishly illustrated history of costume design. Chapters 5 and 6 (pp. 101–156) deal with the Gluck period, with costumes for *Orphée*, *Iphigénie en Aulide*, and *Iphigénie en Tauride*.

535. Horowicz, Bronislaw. *Le théâtre d'opéra*. Paris: Éditions de Flore, 1946. 270 pp. ML1700 H75.

Discusses the relationship between aesthetics and production methods in opera. Extensive references to Gluck, especially pp. 132–143; argues that Gluck had a unique perception of the connection between scenic realism and psychological truth.

536. Nagler, Alois. "Gluck in Wien und Paris." *Maske und Kothurn* 1(1955): 225–267. PN2004 M36.

Investigates productions of Gluck's works from 1753 to the end of the eighteenth century. Cites documentary evidence from a wide range of sources to illuminate the contributions of Gluck's collaborators (designers, choreographers, singers, and instrumentalists) to the realization of his works in the theater.

*Sonnenfels, Joseph von. "Nach der zweiten Vorstellung der *Iphigenie in Tauris*." Cited as item 356.

537. Viale Ferrero, Mercedes. *La scenografia del settecento e i fratelli Galliari*. Turin: Pozzo, 1963. 283 pp. ND2885 V5.

Illustrated in-depth study of Gluck's most famous designers. Useful bibliography on eighteenth-century theater design.

538. ———. "Appunti di scenografia settecentesca, in margine a rappresentazioni di opera in musica di Gluck, e balli di Angiolini." *Chigiana* (item 86): 513–534.

Examines the work of several of Gluck's designers: Bellavite and the brothers Galliari in Milan, Costa in Turin, and Fabrizio Galliari in Parma. Argues that there was a powerful unity of intention harmonizing the work of designer, composer, poet, and choreographer. Fourteen plates.

539. Wolff, Hellmuth Christian. *Oper, Szene und Darstellung von 1600 bis 1900.* (*Musikgeschichte in Bildern* 4/1.) Leipzig: VEB Deutscher Verlag für Musik, 1968. 212 pp. ML89 M9 v4/1.

Lavishly illustrated iconographical study. Perceptive analysis of the history of stage design, dealing in passing with styles of production, singing and dancing, costume, and gesture. The 189 plates also include designs for machinery and views of auditoria. One plate is of a set for *Alceste*, 1776.

540. Zucker, Paul. *Die Theaterdekoration des Klassizismus: eine Kunstgeschichte des Bühnenbildes.* Berlin: Kaemmerer, 1925. 27 pp., 40 plates. PN2091 S8 Z8.

Traces the theory and practice of stage design in the eighteenth century and its development from neoclassical perspective and symmetry to the reshaping of the acting area by the end of the century in pursuit of Romantic ideals. Discusses Goethe's interest in and influence on the Romantic aims of fluidity and asymmetric structures; argues that he had a significant influence on the increasing precision of stage directions.

3. LIBRETTISTS

541. Angermüller, Rudolph. "Reformideen von Du Roullet und Beaumarchais als Opernlibrettisten." *Acta musicologica* 48 (1976): 227–253. ISSN 0001 6241. ML5 I6.

Investigates the genre of *tragédie lyrique* and its traditional libretto; argues that Gluck's reform was closely bound up with the changes to the libretto set forth in Du Roullet's *Lettre sur les drames-opéra* (item 20). Summarizes and comments on this item. Compares Beaumarchais's concept of opera (in *Tarare*) with Du Roullet's. Concludes that the two librettists held parallel but different reform ideas. Both of them advocated classical simplicity, the abandonment of the supernatural, and maintaining the emphasis on words. Beaumarchais, however, was committed to contemporary relevance, while Du Roullet favoured neoclassical subjects and timeless themes. See also Buschmeier (item 423).

542. Baroni, Jole Maria. "La lirica musicale di Metastasio." *Rivista musicale italiana* 12 (1905): 383–406. ML5 R66.

Discusses Metastasio's role as reformer of baroque tradition. Analyzes his use of aria and arietta, and suggests that though his concessions to contemporary taste were not always in the interests of the drama, his sensitivity to musical requirements was unique.

543. Bricqueville, Eugène H. de. *Le livret d'opéra français de Lully à Gluck 1672–1779.* Paris: Maison Schott, 1887. 77 pp.

Analyzes the part played in the evolution of opera by the libretto. Follows Arteaga (item 4) in asserting the decadence of Italian opera despite Metastasio's achievements. Describes Quinault as constrained by convention but more successful than his immediate successors. Argues that Gluck had a unique respect for the libretto, comparing his *Armide* with Lully's. Quotes Gluck's letter to Guillard of June 17, 1778 to show Gluck's intimate involvement with the creation of his librettos. See also Noiray (item 460).

*Buschmeier, Gabriele. " '. . . *de l'emploi du mêtre . . . dépend le grand effet de l'expression musicale'*: Du Roullet, Gluck und die Prosodie." Cited as item 423.

*Calzabigi, Ranieri de'. "Dissertazione di Ranieri de'Calsabigi . . . su le poesie drammatiche del Signor Abate Pietro Metastasio." Cited as item 12.

*———. *Lettre sur le méchanisme de l'opéra italien.* Cited as item 13.

*———. *Risposta . . . alla critica ragionalissima della poesie drammatiche del R. de'Calsabigi.* Cited as item 14.

544. Corte, Andrea della. "Appunti sull'estetica musicale di Pietro Metastasio." *Rivista musicale italiana* 28 (1921): 94–119. ML5 R66.

A response to Rolland (item 561). Refutes Rolland by presenting evidence of Metastasio's fidelity to a traditional view of opera, quoting Metastasio's letters and assessments of his work by his contemporaries, including Burney (item 11), and Arteaga (item 4).

*Du Roullet, François-Louis Gand Leblanc. *Lettre sur les drames-opéra.* Cited as item 20.

545. Einstein, Alfred. "Calzabigi's Erwiderung von 1790." *Gluck-Jahrbuch* 3 (item 87), pp. 25–50.

A commentary on Calzabigi's *Risposta* (item 14). Summarizes the arguments and translates part of the text.

546. Fubini, Enrico. "Presupposti estetici e letterari della riforma di Gluck." *Chigiana* (item 86): 235–245.

Argues that Calzabigi's "Dissertazione" (item 12) implies a covert criticism of Metastasio. Outlines Calzabigi's role in prompting Gluck to respond to a wider range of ideas, particularly from France, conducive to the creation of a new opera type. Assesses how far Gluck responded to Calzabigi's influence.

547. Gallarati, Paolo. "Metastasio e Gluck: per una collocazione storica della riforma" *Chigiana* (item 86): 299–308.

Compares the artistic aims of Gluck and Metastasio. Argues that Gluck built upon Metastasio's reform of the libretto; emphasizes the continuity of Metastasian opera with Gluck's works and the indebtedness of both to a rationalist approach; contests a proto-Romantic interpretation of the reform.

548. ———. "L'estetica musicale di Ranieri de'Calzabigi: la *Lulliade.*" *Nuova rivista musicale italiana* 13 (1979): 531–563. ML5 R66.

Analyzes Calzabigi's aesthetic principles on the basis of his satirical epic (see Muresu, item 556). Concludes that Calzabigi held an ambivalent attitude to the reform and is most accurately seen as a moderate reformer receptive to current ideas of nature and psychological realism but nevertheless steeped in traditional theatrical values.

549. ———. "L'estetica musicale de'Calzabigi: il caso Metastasio." *Nuova rivista musicale italiana* 14 (1980): 497–538. ML5 R66.

Continues the exploration, begun in item 548, of Calzabigi's aesthetic theories; compares them with those of Metastasio; concludes that Metastasio and Calzabigi represent different stages along a continuous historical development that sought to free opera from baroque traditions and create a renewed genre which would restore the vitality and tensions of ancient tragedy.

550. Guiet, René. "L'évolution d'un genre: le livret d'opéra en France de Gluck à la révolution (1774–1793)." *Smith College Studies in Modern Languages* 18 (1936–1937): 1–99. PB13 S6.

Argues that the libretto was uniquely important in France in influencing the development of opera. Identifies two phases of reform, the first beginning c. 1750; cites critical and satirical comment from France and Italy that led to a simplification and rationalization of the genre. Dates the second phrase from Du Roullet's *Iphigénie en Aulide*. Argues that opera had all but replaced tragedy in popular interest by the end of the century; concludes that the libretto reflects all the contradictory trends of end-of-the-century literature.

551. Joly, Jacques. *Les fêtes théâtrales de Métastase à la cour de Vienne (1731–1767)*. Clermont-Ferrand: Faculté des Lettres et Sciences Humaines de l'Université de Clermont-Ferrand, 1978. 525 pp. ISBN X 20 001762 3. ML1723 J6.

Major study of the *festa teatrale* and Metastasio's role in refining and rationalizing the essentially baroque tradition towards the simplicity of plot and musical richness seen in *Orfeo*. See also Sternfeld (item 205), Monelle (item 248), Buschmeier (item 375), Leopold (item 397), Degrada (item 429), and Martina (item 454).

552. Jorgensen, James Lee. "Metastasio: Revaluation and Reformulation." Doctoral dissertation, University of Minnesota, 1980. 285 pp.

553. Lazzeri, Ghino. *La vita e l'opera letteraria di Ranieri Calzabigi: saggio critico con appendice di documenti inediti o rari*. Città di Castello: Lapi, 1907. 220 pp.

Detailed study of Calzabigi's life and works, with extensive coverage of the reform librettos. Examines rival theories concerning the instigation of the reform and argues that Gluck and Calzabigi had complementary roles: Calzabigi as theorist, Gluck as executant.

554. Michel, Hertha. "Ranieri Calzabigi als Dichter von Musikdramen und als Kritiker." *Gluck-Jahrbuch* 4 (item 87): 99–171.

Major study of Calzabigi's life and works. Attempts to assess the degree of Calzabigi's influence over Gluck. (Unfinished because of the discontinuation of the yearbooks.)

555. Monelle, Raymond. "The Rehabilitation of Metastasio." *Music & Letters* 57/2 (1976): 268–291. ISSN 0027 4224. ML5 M64.

Analyzes Metastasio's dramatic technique. Traces changing assessments of his merit from the eighteenth century to the present day. Illustrates his dramatic method with studies of *Demofoonte* and *Ezio*.

556. Muresu, Gabriele. *La ragione dei "Buffoni." La* Lulliade *di Ranieri de' Calzabigi*. Rome: Bulzoni, 1977. 347 pp. PQ4684 C425 L835.

Contains the text of Calzabigi's satirical poem *La Lulliade o I buffi italiani scacciati da Parigi*, with an introductory essay by Muresu. Poem deals with an episode in the Querelle des Bouffons in which an Italian opera company was forced out of Paris by the Lullists. Primary source for Calzabigi's theories on opera, text-setting, and the importance of melody. See Gallarati (item 548).

557. Prod'homme, Jacques-Gabriel. "Note sur deux librettistes français de Gluck: Du Roullet et Moline. (D'après des documents inédits.)" *Zeitschrift der Internationalen Musikgesellschaft* 7 (1905–1906): 12–15. ML5 I68.

Cites documents from the lives of Du Roullet and Moline, including baptismal registers. Gives brief, factual summary of their association with Gluck.

558. ———. "Gluck's French Collaborators." Trans. Marguerite Barton. *The Musical Quarterly* 3 (1917): 249–271. ISSN 0027 4631. ML1 M725. The same material appears in French in *Le ménestrel* 53 (1926): 557–559; 13–15 (1928): 141–143, 153–155, 165–166. ML5 M465.

Deals briefly with the careers of Du Roullet, Moline, and de Tschoudi. Quotes letters and documents from Gluck's Paris years and aims to assess the contribution of these librettists to the reform.

559. ———. "Deux collaborateurs italiens de Gluck." *Rivista musicale italiana* 23 (1916): 33–65, 201–218. ML5 R66. Reprinted in *Le ménestrel* 27–29 (1928): 301–303, 313–316, 325–327; and 38–40 (1928): 397–399, 405–407, 413–414. ML5 M465.

Part One describes Calzabigi's career, examining both his commercial and artistic enterprises. Part Two investigates the impresario Count Giuseppe Maratti d'Affligio (d'Afflisio), whose connections with Gluck were nearly financially disastrous for the composer. For a more recent study of Gluck and d'Afflisio, see Grossegger (item 116).

560. Robinson, Michael. "The Ancient and the Modern: A Comparison of Metastasio and Calzabigi." *Studies in Music* 7 (1982): 137–147. ISSN 0081 8267. ML5 S9255.

Argues that during Calzabigi's working life, the libretto came to be regarded as a genre distinct from spoken drama; his aims were therefore different from Metastasio's. His greatest achievement was the creation of the tableau, incorporating the pictorial into the musico-literary genre. In Metastasian opera, love is portrayed as a disturbing element, disordering the world; in Calzabigi's operas love rules, bringing a new order.

561. Rolland, Romain. "Métastase, précurseur de Gluck." *Revue musicale de la Société Internationale de Musique* 8/4 (1912): 1–10. Reprinted in *Voyage musical au pays du passé*. Paris: Joseph 1919, reprinted Hachette, 1920, pp. 157–177. ML390 R67.

Argues that Metastasio's role in the reform has been underestimated. Identifies his contribution as comprising the reintroduction of the chorus and the establishment of a balance between *secco* and *accompagnato* recitative. Discusses Metastasio's letter to Hasse of October 20, 1749 which contains specific requests for *accompagnati*, orchestral passages, and a final chorus "to form a necessary part of the tragic catastrophe." But see della Corte (item 544).

562. Smith, Patrick J. *The Tenth Muse. A Historical Study of the Opera Libretto.* London: Gollancz, 1971. xvi 417, pp. ISBN 0 575 00669 2. ML2110 S62.

Wide-ranging though somewhat superficial survey. Chapter 9 deals with Gluck and Calzabigi; Chapter 10 discusses Gluck and his French librettists.

563. Welti, Heinrich. "Gluck and Calsabigi." *Vierteljahrschrift für Musikwissenschaft* 7 (1891): 26–42. ML5 V5.

Sifts documentary evidence to evaluate the relationship between Gluck and Calzabigi.

4. SINGERS

*Abert, Hermann. *"Zu Glucks Ippolito."* Cited as item 368.

564. Cattelan, Paolo. "La musica della 'omnigena religio': accademie musicali a Padova nel secondo settecento." *Acta musicologica* 59/2 (1987): 152–186. ISSN 0001 6241. ML5 I6.

Traces Guadagni's role in the dramatic performances given in the Masonic circle of Giuseppe Ximenes in Padua. Argues that through the influence of this circle, Guadagni came to identify with the role of Orpheus, exaggerating its static, archaic, mystical interpretation.

565. ———. "Altri Orfei di Gaetano Guadagni: dai pasticci al nuovo *Orfeo* di Bertoni." Preface to Ferdinando Bertoni, *Orfeo ed Euridice*, ed. Cattelan. Milan: Ricordi, 1989, pp. ix–cxliv. ISBN 88 7592 074 5.

Major study of the part played by Guadagni in the dissemination and transformation of *Orfeo*. Argues that Guadagni's concept of the opera was different from Gluck's and that he viewed the opera as a kind of oratorio or "*azione sacra.*" Notes Guadagni's role in *pasticcios* in London, Munich, Florence, and Padua (with table comparing the texts of the different versions, pp. xxvi–xliv). Argues that a major influence on Guadagni was the academy of Giuseppe Ximenes d'Aragona in Padua, and that this influence, transmitted by Guadagni to Bertoni, can be seen in Bertoni's setting of Calzabigi's libretto, performed in Venice in 1776.

*Corri, Domenico. *A Select Collection of the Most Admired Songs, Duetts etc. from Operas in the Highest Esteem.* Cited as item 303.

566. Finscher, Ludwig. "Der Opernsänger als Komponist. Giuseppe Millico und seine Oper *La pietà d'amore.*" *Opernstudien Anna Amalie Abert zum 65. Geburstag,* ed. Klaus Hortschansky. Tutzing: Schneider, 1975, pp. 57–90. ISBN 3 7952 0155 1. ML55 A15 1975.

Investigates the life of one of Gluck's favorite singers. Includes an account of his opera *La pietà d'amore* with extensive music examples.

567. Foucher, Paul. "Les cantatrices dramatiques: Catarina Gabrielli." *Chronique musicale* 6 (1874): 164–170, 261–267; 7 (1875): 19–24. ML5 C56.

Anecdotal biography of the singer who created the roles of Nice in *La danza*, Claudia in *L'innocenza giustificata*, Elisa in *Il re pastore*, and the title role in *Tetide*.

568. Heriot, Angus. *The Castrati in Opera.* London: Secker & Warburg, 1956. 243 pp. ML400 H47.

Written for the general reader, but containing biographical information not readily available elsewhere. Sections on Guadagni, Millico, and Tenducci.

569. Howard, Patricia. "Did Burney Blunder?" *The Musical Times* 139 (1998): 29–32. ISSN 0027 4666. ML5 M85.

Compares conflicting descriptions of the voice of Gaetano Guadagni. Refutes Burney's claim that Guadagni changed from alto to soprano register in later life, arguing that the singer's available range was unchanging, differing with genre and repertory rather than with age.

570. ———. "Guadagni in the Dock." *Early Music* 27/1 (1999): 87–95. ISSN 0306 1078. ML5 E18.

Examines the incident in which Gaetano Guadagni was brought to trial for singing in an opera performance considered illegal in the light of the Licensing Act of 1737.

571. ———. " 'Mr Justice Blindman' and the 'Priestess of Fashion.' " *Il Saggiatore musicale* 7/1 (2000): 47–59. ISSN 1123 8615. ML5 S137.

Develops the investigation in item 570, focusing on the role of Sir John Fielding in prosecuting infringements of the Licensing Act of 1737 and the attempts of Teresa Cornelys to circumvent it.

572. Prod'homme, Jacques-Gabriel. "Rosalie Levasseur, Ambassadress of Opera." Trans. Julia Gregory. *The Musical Quarterly* 2 (1916): 210–243. ISSN 0027 4631. ML1 M725.

An account of the career of the singer (and mistress of the Austrian ambassador in Paris) who created the role of Amour in *Orphée* and took over the role of *Iphigénie* from Sophie Arnould in the 1775 production of *Iphigénie en Aulide*. Explores her creation of the title roles in *Alceste*, *Armide*, and *Iphigénie en Tauride*.

573. Rogers, Francis. "Sophie Arnould (1740–1803)" *The Musical Quarterly* 4 (1920): 57–61. ISSN 0027 4631. ML1 M725.

Brief account of the career of Arnould as courtesan and creator of the title role in *Iphigénie en Aulide*. Notes Garrick's approval of her acting and attributes her success, which was achieved despite her small voice, to her superb diction and acting.

574. Waddington, Patrick. "Pauline Viardot-Garcia as Berlioz's Counselor and Physician." *The Musical Quarterly* 59 (1973): 382–398. ISSN 0027 4631. ML1 M725.

Deals with the relationship between Viardot-Garcia and Berlioz and her role in the revision of *Orphée* for Paris in 1859. See Fauquet (item 309).

5. PRODUCTION ISSUES, THEATER ADMINISTRATION, AND ARCHIVES

575. Angermüller, Rudolph. "Opernreform im Lichte der wirtschaftlichen Verhältnis an der Académie Royal de Musique von 1775 bis 1780." *Die Musikforschung* 25 (1972): 267–291. ISSN 0027 4801. ML5 M9437.

From a study of the accounts of the Paris Opéra, argues that Gluck's operas saved the Académie from financial disaster.

*————. "Kassenschlager Gluck an der Pariser Académie Royale de Musique." Cited as item 278.

576. Barthélemy, Maurice. "Les règlements de 1776 et l'Académie Royal de Musique." *Recherches sur la musique classique français* 4 (1964): 239–248. ISSN 0080 0139. ML270 R43.

Examines the state of crisis at the Opéra in 1776 and the steps taken to remedy the financial deficit and improve morale. Touches on the part played by Gluck's operas, especially *Alceste*, in restoring confidence in the administration.

577. Croce, Benedetto. *I teatre di Napoli, secolo XV–XVIII*. Naples: Pierro, 1891. xi, 786 pp. PN2686 N3 C7.

Archival history with useful documentary sources on the performances of *La clemenza di Tito* in Naples in 1752 (pp. 437–439).

578. Framery, Nicolas Etienne and Pierre Louis Ginguéné. *Encyclopédie méthodique: Musique*, vol. 1. Paris: Panckoucke, 1791.

Among a collection of miscellaneous articles on music, includes a brief but specific account of Gluck's method of directing the chorus and ballet in *Iphigénie en Aulide* (pp. 270–271).

579. Gotti, T. "Bologna musicale del 1700 e Cristoforo Gluck." *Due secoli di vita musicale: storia del Teatro Communale di Bologna*, ed. Lamberto Trezzini. Bologna: Edizioni Alfa, 1966, vol. 1, pp. 45–78. ML1733 8 B442 T43.

Documentary study of Gluck's work at the Teatro Communale and the first performances of *Il trionfo di Clelia* in 1763.

580. Heartz, Daniel. "Nicolas Jadot and the Building of the Burgtheater." *The Musical Quarterly* 68/1 (1982): 1–31. ISSN 0027 4631. ML1 M725.

Traces the building and subsequent remodelling of the Burgtheater from 1741 to the end of the century. Many illustrations and diagrams.

*Mairobert, Mathieu François Pidansat de. "Lettre XIV. Sur l'Opéra." Cited as item 339.

581. Michtner, Otto. *Das alte Burgtheater als Opernbühne.* (*Theatergeschichte Österreichs*, vol. 3, part 1.) Vienna: Böhlaus, 1970. 566 pp. ISBN 3 205 03204 7. PN2610 T5 3/1.

Archival study of the repertory of the Burgtheater between 1778 and 1792. Includes lists of singers and operas.

582. Mueller [Müller] von Asow, Erich Hermann. *Die Mingottischen Opern Unternehmungen 1732–1756.* Dresden: Hille, 1915, xiv, 123, ccxiii pp. ML1703 M93 1915. 2nd ed., as *Angelo und Pietro Mingotti: ein Beitrag zur Geschichte der Oper im XVIII. Jahrhundert.* Dresden: Bertling, 1917. xvii, 141, cccx pp. ML1703 M93 1917.

Documentary study establishing the constitution and repertory of the company and providing evidence of Gluck's involvement; 2nd ed. has indexes of single arias mentioned and index of composers. See also Müller, item 135.

583. Paglicci Brozzi, Antonio. *Il Regio Ducal Teatro di Milano nel secolo XVIII.* Milan: Ricordi, 1894. 129 pp. ML1733 8 M5 P3.

Archival study of the theater that housed Gluck's earliest operas. Detailed index of repertory.

584. Prod'homme, Jacques-Gabriel. *L'Opéra (1669–1925)*. Paris: Delagrave, 1925. xvi, 165 pp. ML1727 8 P2 P8.

Sourcebook of documentary information on the administration and repertory of the Opéra.

*Prota-Giurleo, Ulisse. "Notizie biografiche intorno ad alcuni musicisti d'oltralpe a Napoli nel settecento." Cited as item 138.

585. Puncuh, Dino. "Giacomo Durazzo—famiglia, ambiente, personalità." *Gluck in Wien* (item 81), pp. 69–77.

Biographical sketch of the theater director who brought about the *Orfeo* collaboration, by the archivist of the Durazzo family papers.

586. Ricci, Corrado. *I teatri di Bologna nei secoli XVII e XVIII*. Bologna: Monti, 1888. xxxi, 736 pp. PN2686 B6 R5.

Documentary history. Includes references to *Demofoonte*, *La Semiramide riconosciuta*, *Il re pastore* and *Orfeo*, with more fully documented accounts of *Il trionfo di Clelia* and *Alceste*. Important appendix (pp. 625–644) reproducing Calzabigi's detailed instructions for the staging *Alceste* in 1778, including his direction that the corps de ballet and the chorus should be merged, with the chorus using expressive gesture as they had done in Vienna. See, however, Betzwieser (item 164).

587. Sehnal, Jirí. "Gluck im Repertoire des Schlosstheaters des Grafen Haugwitz in Námest nad Oslavou." *Gluck in Wien* (item 81), pp. 171–177.

Gives details of a collection of Gluck scores, many in manuscript, identifying the repertory performed at the Schlosstheater, and currently held in the Moravian Museum, Brno (CZ-Bm).

*Teneo, Martial. "Les chefs-d'œuvre du Chevalier Gluck à l'Opéra de Paris." Cited as item 479.

588. Zechmeister, Gustav. *Die Wiener Theatre nächst der Burg und nächst dem Kärntnerthor von 1747 bis 1776.* (*Theatergeschichte Österreichs*, vol. 3, part 2.) Vienna: Böhlaus, 1971. 632 pp. ISBN 3 205 03205 5. PN2610 T5 3/2.

Archival study of the repertory of opera, ballet, and spoken drama. Some inaccuracies (e.g., includes the supposed performance of *Orfeo* at Joseph II's coronation in 1764) but with generally useful appendices listing directors and programs.

VIII

Indexes

1. AUTHOR INDEX

Numbers refer to item numbers in the bibliography.

Gottsched, Johann Christoph, 21
Grétry, André Ernest Modeste, 115
Grimm, Friedrich Melchior, 22, 321
Grossegger, Elisabeth, 116, 322
Gruber, Gernot, 241, 514, 515
Gugler, Bernhard, 386
Guiet, René, 550

Haas, Robert, 323, 387, 494, 516, 528
Hammelman, Hans, 53
Hammerich, Angul, 134
Hammond, Tom, 444
Hastings, Margaret, 438
Hayes, Jeremy, 439
Heartz, Daniel, 117, 118, 119, 242, 440, 580
Heckmann, Herbert, 24
Henzel, Christoph, 325
Heriot, Angus, 568
Hoffmann, Ernst Theodor Wilhelm, 326
Holzer, Ludmilla, 495
Hopkinson, Cecil, 43
Horowicz, Bronislaw, 535
Hortschansky, Klaus, 54, 55, 83, 120, 178, 179, 388, 389, 390, 391, 392, 393
Howard, Patricia, 56, 57, 121, 180, 441, 442, 443, 444, 445, 446, 447, 502, 569, 570, 571

Istel, Edgar, 181

Jäger, Erich, 243
Joly, Jacques, 394, 448, 551
Jorgensen, James Lee, 552
Jullien, Adolphe, 449

Kantner, Leopold M., 327
Kaplan, James Maurice, 58
Karro, Françoise, 122
Kaufmann, Harald, 182, 183
Keller, Otto, 44

Kelly, Michael, 23
Khevenhüller-Metsch, Johann Josef, 24
Kinsky, Georg, 59, 123
Kirk, Elise K., 244
Kling, H., 124
Klinger, Kurt, 184
Kohut, Adolph, 245
Koller, Walter, 185
Komorn, Maria, 60
Kraeft, Kay Kathleen, 395
Kratochwill, Max, 125
Kretzschmar, Hermann, 126, 328, 329, 503
Krüger, Manfred, 529
Kunze, Stefan, 330
Kurth, Ernst, 396

La Harpe, Jean-François de, 331, 332, 333, 334
La Laurencie, Lionel de, 127, 450
La Mara, *see under* Lipsius
Landon, H. C. Robbins, 186
Landormy, Paul, 128
LaRue, Jan, 523
Lavoix, Henri, 187
Lazzeri, Ghino, 553
Le Blond, Gaspard Michel, 335
Lederer, Josef-Horst, 517
Leopold, Silke, 397
Leroux, Jean, 70
Lesure, François, 45, 336
Liebeskind, Josef, 49
Lipsius, Ida Maria (La Mara), 129, 524
Liszt, Franz, 337
Lockspeiser, Edward, 338
Löwenbach, Jan, 134
Loewenberg, Alfred, 451
Long, [Mademoiselle], 134
Longyear, R. Morgan, 246
Loppert, Max, 398, 452
Luca, Ignaz de, 130
Lynham, Deryck, 530

Wolff, Hellmuth Christian, 539
Wörner, Karl, 367
Wortsmann, Stephan, 48
Wotquenne, Alfred, 49
Würtz, Roland, 216
Wurtzbach, Constantin, 50

Yorke-Long, Alan, 275

Zechmeister, Gustav, 588
Zucker, Paul, 540

2. INDEX OF COMPOSITIONS BY GLUCK

The number in square brackets after a title refers to its place in the list of Gluck's compositions in Chapter I, where included. Other numbers refer to item numbers.

Achille, [77], 522
Alceste (1767), [38], 33, 53, 62, 64, 85,
    105, 130, 138, 150, 165, 173, 175, 177,
    182, 185, 188, 189, 235, 237, 246, 299,
    311, 312, 342, 348, 357, 370, 405, 406,
    408, 424, 432, 442, 443, 452, 463, 464,
    477, 586
Alceste (1776), [45], 85, 162, 163, 173,
    175, 188, 199, 237, 281, 293, 294, 301,
    316, 339, 345, 416, 417, 418, 424, 432,
    438, 442, 443, 452, 471, 477, 533, 539,
    572
Alessandro, see under *Les amours
    d'Alexandre et de Roxane*
Les amours champêtres, see under *Die
    Maienkönigin*
*Les amours d'Alexandre et de Roxane
    (Alessandro)*, [74], 383, 522
Les amours de Flore et Zéphire, [69], 509
Antigono, [20], 224, 369, 409
Arianna, [54], 391
Armide, [46], 45, 165, 175, 185, 282, 283,
    301, 308, 334, 346, 347, 367, 415, 422,
    436, 439, 445, 533, 572
Arsace, [50], 138, 388, 392, 400
Artamene, [10], 106, 373
Artaserse, [1], 370, 371

Le cadi dupé, [29], 216, 491, 496
La caduta de'giganti, [9], 106, 373
Le cinesi, [17], 104, 382, 394, 395, 397,
    398
La Citera assiedata, [73], 103
La clemenza di Tito, [16], 138, 199, 254,
    403, 404, 460, 577
La contesa de'numi, [13], 227
La corona, [36], 377, 389, 399
La Cythère assiégée (1759), [24], 390,
    487, 497
La Cythère assiégée (1775), [44], 52, 487,
    525

La danza, [18], 38, 383, 401, 567
Demetrio, [2], 370
Demofoonte, [3], 38, 254, 262, 392, 555,
    586
De profundis, [68], 143, 194, 500, 502,
    504
Don Juan, [72], 103, 166, 199, 506, 508,
    511, 513, 514, 516, 518, 519

Écho et Narcisse, [48], 213, 285, 286, 430,
    467, 479, 481, 482
Ezio (1750), [14], 211, 374, 386, 403, 409,
    555